≈ ESOTERIC DEVELOPMENT

Esoteric Development

Selected Lectures and Writings

RUDOLF STEINER

SteinerBooks

Published by SteinerBooks
P.O. Box 799
Great Barrington, MA 01230
www.steinerbooks.org

This edition by SteinerBooks, copyright © 2003
Introduction by Stephen E. Usher copyright ©2003

Library of Congress Cataloging-in-Publication Data

Steiner, Rudolf, 1861–1925.
  Esoteric development : lectures and writings / Rudolf Steiner.— Rev. ed.
    p. cm.
  Includes bibliographical references.
  ISBN 0-88010-524-0 (alk. paper)
  1. Anthroposophy. I. Title.
BP595 .S848 2003
299'.935—dc21
                                                                2003012453

Printed in the United States of America

CONTENTS

Introduction

Stephen E. Usher

Esoteric Development and Spiritual Research

"Esoteric development," the theme of this volume, refers to the systematic development of capacities latent in the human being that, when carried far enough, lead to direct experience of spiritual reality, experience that is not accessible to the physical senses and the intellect that is bound to them. It follows that esoteric development leads to experiences beyond the scope of natural science. Esoteric development might be compared to embryological development with the difference that embryological development occurs unconsciously and at the physical level while esoteric development is guided consciously by the individual and occurs, at least in the initial phases, in the soul. The first selection of this volume is a lecture titled "Inner Development" (December 7, 1905, Berlin), which means the same thing as "esoteric development." There it is stated that inner development "refers to the ascent of the human being to capacities which must be acquired if he wishes to make supersensible insights his own."

The volume consists of two articles and eight lectures by Rudolf Steiner, written or delivered between 1905 and 1923. In the sixth selection, "The Great Initiates," Steiner speaks of never setting "limits on our capacity to know, seeing it instead as something to be both widened and uplifted." He also observes in this lecture of March 16, 1905 (Berlin), that it is the greatest arrogance to regard one's own capacity for knowledge as if it were decisive and to declare that it is not possible to transcend it. Steiner was fully aware of the difficulties caused by this arrogance, because he had developed his own capacities for knowledge to a level that towered far above those typical of the most gifted representatives of his time, and those of his time largely refused to recognize what Steiner had to offer.

Steiner was, indeed, a great initiate who had traveled far along the path of esoteric development and was, consequently, eminently qualified to describe the exercises, disciplines, and practices that a student of higher knowledge needs for his own esoteric striving. In "The Great Initiates," Steiner speaks of "teachers who experienced each school, devoted themselves to every exercise, and truly contemplated each step and every level. We should entrust ourselves only to such teachers of initiation schools." The modern aspirant to esoteric development cannot do better than entrust himself to Rudolf Steiner who through his published writings and lectures stands as the greatest teacher of the modern, western path of inner development.

In "The Great Initiates," Steiner describes the relation between a modern esoteric teacher and student by explaining that nothing of "authority" or "dogmatism" is involved, only the giving of counsel and advice. The relation is one based on trust. ("What is necessary is simply that there be trust between pupil and teacher in this sphere.") In the preface to the 1914 edition of *How Does One Attain Knowledge of Higher Worlds?*[1]

---

1. The actual English title to this book is: *How to Know Higher Worlds* or *Knowledge of Higher Worlds and Its Attainment*. Both are incorrect translations of the German, *Wie erlangt man Erkenntnisse der höheren Weten?* The correct translation is as indicated.

Steiner—contrasting the situation in 1914 to the time of the
first appearance of the book, 1904–1905—again discussed the
relation between the teacher and pupil of esoteric development:[1]

> At that time I had to explain that a great deal of what was
> not yet described in the book could be learned by oral com-
> munication. Much of this material has since been published.
> But allusions to it before publication left the possibility of
> misinterpretation and misunderstanding on the part of the
> reader. It might be possible, for instance, to imagine some-
> thing much more vital in the personal relations between the

---

1. It should be noted that only the Western spiritual research is capable of a
fruitful complimentary interaction with natural science. See Rudolf Steiner, *Correspondence and Documents, 1901–1925,* "Notes by Rudolf Steiner written for
Edouard Schuré in Barr, Alsace, September 1907," particularly part III, pp. 9–
19. "It should be understood that the introduction of a correct esotericism in the
West can only be of the Rosicrucian-Christian type, because this *latter* gave birth
to Western life and because by its loss mankind would deny the meaning and
destiny of the Earth. The harmonious relationship between science and religion
can flower only in this esotericism, while every amalgamation of Western knowledge and Eastern esotericism can only produce such unproductive mongrels as
Sinnett's *Esoteric Buddhism.*"
   On the relation between the Eastern and Western Schools of esoteric development, see *From the History and Contents of the First Section of the Esoteric School
1904–1914,* pp. 314–315: "Previously the Western School was only an append-
age to the Eastern one, was subordinate to it; now, however, both are simply
linked by a bond of brotherhood, each going its separate way, independent of
one another. The Western School is no longer subordinate to the Eastern
School, but they are coordinated.... The Christian teaching and the Christian-
Rosicrucian teaching now exist in the West. The former educates through feelings, the latter though understanding. The dying cultures of the East still need
the Eastern teachings. The Western teachings are for future cultures.... One of
these schools is led by Mrs. Besant, the other by Dr. Steiner. But we have to
decide which one to follow." The text also names the great Eastern Masters who
stood behind Mrs. Besant and the great Western Masters who stood behind
Rudolf Steiner.

seeker for spiritual schooling and this or that teacher than is intended. I trust I have here succeeded, by presenting details in a certain way, in emphasizing more strongly that for one seeking spiritual schooling in accord with present spiritual conditions an absolute direct relation to the objective spiritual world is of far greater importance than a relation to the personality of a teacher. The latter will gradually become merely the helper; he will assume the same position in spiritual schooling as a teacher occupies, in conformity with modern views, in any other field of knowledge. I believe I have sufficiently stressed the fact that the teacher's authority and the pupil's faith in him should play no greater part in spiritual schooling than in any other branch of knowledge or life. A great deal depends, it seems to me, upon an increasing true estimate of this relation between the one who carries on *spiritual research* and those who develop an interest in the results of his research. [emphasis added]

The last sentence quoted above refers to spiritual research. The idea of spiritual research is one of Steiner's seminal thoughts. What Steiner indicates with this concept is the possibility of a new form of science, a science of the spirit that complements the natural science that burst in upon human evolution around A.D. 1500 with the great discoveries associated with names like Copernicus, Kepler, Tycho Brahe, and so on. Steiner explains and defends this idea and the possibility of spiritual research in the second selection in this volume, "The Psychological Basis of Spiritual Science," the text of a lecture that he delivered to a congress of philosophers on April 11, 1911, in Bologna. There he articulates the view that the human being can undergo a systematic development of his faculties of soul and spirit through special exercises and, thereby, new experiences are opened up, experiences that are not accessible to the methods of natural science and are the domain of spiritual research:

> These exercises have an intimate soul character and take a unique form in each person. Once we have begun, the element of individuality results from the way each soul is used in practicing the exercises. What always follows, however, is a positive awareness of living in a reality that is suprasensory in nature and independent of one's outer physical body. For the sake of simplicity, let us refer to one who is looking for these soul experiences as a "spiritual researcher" [*Geistesforscher*]. For a spiritual researcher there is a definite awareness, in complete presence of mind, that behind the bodily organization perceptible to the senses there is a suprasensory organization. There is an awareness that it is possible to experience oneself within this suprasensory organization just as normal consciousness is aware of itself within the physical body.

Later in this same lecture Steiner describes how spiritual research and natural scientific research are really complimentary endeavors indicating how they can both explore aspects of the same reality:[1]

> One would have to see that the ordinary empirical content of consciousness is related to what is truly experienced in the inner life of one's core being, just as a mirrored image is related to the real being of the person viewed in a mirror.

---

1. This is GA 25 in the German complete works. It is an essay written at the time of the so-called French course, *Philosophy, Cosmology, Religion* in 1922.

By thinking in this way in relation to the theory of knowledge, conflict could certainly be eliminated between natural science, with its inclination toward materialism, and spiritual research, which presupposes the spiritual....

[It can be seen] in all of what natural science can establish, the idea mentioned (which is fundamental from the perspective of epistemology) sees only those arrangements that *reflect* the true core of the human being. This core of being, however, is not located within the physical organization, but in the transcendental. Spiritual research should thus be thought of as a way to gain knowledge of the true nature of the phenomenon reflected. Obviously, the basis of all the laws of the physical organism and those of the suprasensory would be behind this antithesis, or *being* and *mirror.*

None of this, however, is any disadvantage to one's practice of the scientific method from either direction. By maintaining this antithesis, the method would, as it were, flow into two currents that mutually illuminate and clarify each other. For it must be said that the physical organization is not a mere reflector in an absolute sense, independent of the suprasensory. After all, the reflector must be seen as the product of the suprasensory being mirrored by it. (emphasis added)

The two currents are evidently spiritual scientific research and natural scientific research.

In the lecture "Suprasensory Knowledge," delivered on September 26, 1923, in Vienna (third selection), Steiner describes how the scientific method, established by natural science is related to spiritual scientific research. The spiritual researcher

xii ESOTERIC DEVELOPMENT

uses a scientific method to develop his own faculties to the point where he can make specific observations in the spiritual world. It is the process of esoteric development, in other words, that is pursued scientifically. Once the higher faculties are sufficiently developed certain spiritual phenomena can be observed and as the development continues further phenomena come into view:

A natural scientist applies this precision to external experimentation and observation, hoping to see things juxtaposed so that they reveal their secrets with exactness in the process of quantification. Spiritual scientists, of whom I am speaking, apply this precision to the development of their own soul forces. To use an expression of Goethe, their inner discovery, through which the spirit world and human immortality step before one's soul, is made in a precise way. With every step of a spiritual scientist toward revealing the spiritual world to the eyes of the soul, one feels obligated to perceive conscientiously, just as a mathematician must at every step. And just as mathematicians must see clearly into everything they write down, spiritual scientists likewise look with absolute precision at everything they uncover through powers of cognition. They understand that they have developed the soul's eye from the soul itself, using the same inner laws that nature uses to form physical eyes from bodily substance. They know they can speak of spirit worlds with the same authority one uses when speaking of the sensory world seen with physical eyes. In this sense, the spiritual research we are discussing satisfies the requirements of the magnificent achievements of natural science—which spiritual science in no way opposes, but seeks to supplement.

From this last passage one can see that Steiner is speaking about an exacting scientific method of esoteric development. This method leads to accurate spiritual scientific observations of spiritual phenomena. It is worth underscoring that this scientific exactness is essential, for what the student is actually doing is bringing his own higher being to birth and endowing it with organs of supersensible perception. Lack of precise work can lead to an unhealthy entry into the spiritual world and inaccurate observations. As Steiner explained in "Three Decisions on the Path of Imagination Knowledge: Loneliness, Fear, and Dread" (lecture of March 2, 1915 in Berlin and last selection in this volume): The question most people ask "is not whether they enter the spirit world in the correct way, but whether they enter it at all." The scientific method of esoteric development described by Rudolf Steiner insures proper entry into the spiritual world.

It also should be grasped that Steiner viewed the emergence of a real science of the spirit based on spiritual research as essential to the future evolution of humanity. Indeed, it is stated in the third statute of the Anthroposophical Society, founded by Rudolf Steiner and his associates in 1923 at the Christmas Conference in Dornach, Switzerland:

> These results [of spiritual research] are in their own way as exact as the results of genuine natural science. When the former attain general recognition in the same way as the latter, they will bring about comparable progress in all spheres of life, not only in the spiritual but also in the practical realm.

Rudolf Steiner's Primary Works on Esoteric Development

The material in this volume supplements and augments other works of Steiner on the theme of esoteric development and spiritual research. His fundamental and basic work on the theme is *How Does One Attain Knowledge of Higher Worlds?* Other important written works about the path of inner development are as follows:

Theosophy
An Outline of Esoteric Science
The Stages of Higher Knowledge
A Way of Self Knowledge
On the Life of the Soul
Philosophy, Cosmology, & Religion[1]

Further works on the theme by Rudolf Steiner include:

Guidance in Esoteric Training
From the History and Contents of the First Section of the
  Esoteric School, 1904–1914

Also of great importance are Steiner's four "Mystery" dramas, four plays that depict the lives of a group of individuals who are actively engaged in esoteric development. The dramas, published under the title *Four Mystery Dramas,* present, if you will, case histories of esoteric development. These make clear the diverse and often complex byways that an individual's development can take and therefore the plays provide an

---

1. It is this writer's understanding that what is not revealed in these published works of Rudolf Steiner about esoteric development will be revealed to the pupil by a teacher or initiate, either living or disincarnate, when one has mastered what has been published.

important complement to the more textbook perfect case of esoteric development described in Steiner's books and lectures on esoteric development.

While the Mystery Dramas present case histories and the works listed above present the general path of esoteric development Steiner also gave advice regarding the esoteric development of people engaged in the various professions. In the cycle called *Course for Young Doctors*, Steiner gave specific advice regarding the esoteric development of medical doctors. In *Curative Education* Steiner makes suggestions regarding the esoteric path for those working with people with special needs. The volume *The Boundaries of Natural Science* speaks of a path specialized to natural scientists. The School for Spiritual Science that Steiner inaugurated at the same time that he re-founded the Anthroposophical Society—the Christmas Foundation meeting of 1923—was formed with sections for different areas of scientific and artistic inquiry. It was evidently Steiner's intention to create specialized paths of esoteric development for each of these professions to be taught in the respective sections. The idea was to tailor the path for the specific spiritual research requirements of the different professions. These specialized indications should be viewed as a complement to the more general material.

Generally speaking, thoughts on esoteric development are scattered throughout Steiner's complete works comprising over 360 volumes.

The content of this volume together with the material mentioned above constitutes a comprehensive look at esoteric development. It reveals both what the individual wishing such a development must undertake to bring it about and what he will experience along the way. This material is also valuable to

xvi ·· E S O T E R I C D E V E L O P M E N T

the student of spiritual science not interested in undertaking a path of inner development. It answers the question of how spiritual scientific knowledge is discovered.

In "The Rosicrucian Spiritual Path" (Oct. 20, 1906, seventh selection) Steiner explains that if this trust is lost, "the essential bond would be torn apart, and the forces at play between teacher and student would cease to be effective." Two observations are in order regarding this statement. First, the reader may see a contradiction between this reference to an "essential bond" and "forces at play" between them, on the one hand, and Steiner's statement from the 1914 preface to *How Does One Attain Knowledge of Higher Worlds?* (quoted next in this introduction) on the other. In the preface, Steiner states:

> It might be possible, for instance, to imagine something much more vital in the personal relations between the seeker for spiritual schooling and this or that teacher than is intended.

The point is that one could take a "special bond" or "forces which play between them" as being exactly the "something more vital" that Steiner says does not exist. This writer's understanding of the distinction is that the bond in the more ancient methods of spiritual schooling were "more vital," inasmuch as a kind of direct working on the student's subtle bodies was carried out by the teacher. Such a relation would be totally inappropriate today, at least in the West, as it would be incompatible with freedom. The modern teacher works in a fashion similar to that of a teacher of mathematics. There something remarkable does occur as explained by Rudolf Steiner in the appendix to the 1918 edition of his *Philosophy of Spiritual Activity.* Speaking of what happens when we encounter another human being who is expressing his thoughts, Steiner states the sense perception we have of this other (e.g. a teacher of mathematics),

> Through the thinking with which I confront the other person, the percept of him becomes, as it were, transparent to the mind. I am bound to admit that when I grasp the percept with my thinking, it is not at all the same thing as appeared to the outer senses. In what is a direct appearance to the senses, something else is indirectly revealed. The mere sense appearance extinguishes itself at the same time as it confronts me. But what it reveals through this extinguishing compels me as a thinking being to extinguish my own thinking as long as I am under its influence, and to put its thinking in the place of mine. I then grasp its thinking in my thinking as an experience like my own. I have really perceived another person's thinking. The immediate percept, extinguishing itself as sense appearance, is grasped by my thinking, and this is a process lying wholly within my consciousness and consisting in this, that the other person's thinking takes the place of mine. Through the self-extinction of the sense appearance, the separation between the two spheres of consciousness is actually overcome.

When the other person is a trusted spiritual teacher, the pupil experiences the teacher's thoughts as his own, thus receiving his council and advice. With more or, perhaps better said, different effort a student can gain this advice and counsel from the published works of Rudolf Steiner.

The second point is that the phrase "torn apart" quoted at the beginning of this note was mistranslated as "ruptured" in the first edition of this book. Another translation error occurred in the first edition of the fifth selection, "General

Requirements for Esoteric Development." In this selection the "six exercises" are described in a unique way, inasmuch as the description of each exercise ends with instructions on how to direct certain currents in the body. The translation error concerns the description of the second of the six exercises. The late Gisele O'Neil pointed out to me that the German original phrase, *"dass man es von Kopfe bis über das Herz herabströmen lasse,"* is correctly translated "that one let it stream from the head down and around the heart." The first edition incorrectly translates this "letting it stream down from the head to a point just above the heart." This is obviously an important distinction for anyone attempting to practice the exercise. The same error occurs in the book, *Guidance in Esoteric Training,* which also presents a translation of this text. These comments are not intended as criticism of the translators who have generally done good work, but rather to inform readers of these two problems.

1. Esoteric Development

Concepts of the suprasensory world and its relationship to the sensory world have been discussed here in a long series of lectures. It is only natural that this question should come up repeatedly: "Where does knowledge of suprasensory world come from?" Today we will address this question, which is really a question of inner human development.

Here, the term "inner development" means that one rises to the individual capacities needed to gain suprasensory understanding. Do not misunderstand the intention of this lecture. We will in no way stipulate rules or laws of general human morality, nor will we challenge modern religion in general. I have to emphasize this, because whenever esotericism is discussed, a misunderstanding often arises, and it is believed that some sort of general requirements or dogmatic moral rules are being established. This is not the case. This point must become particularly clear in our age of standardization, which always fails to recognize individual differences among human beings. Neither should this lecture be assumed to be about the fundamentals of the anthroposophic movement.[1] Esotericism is not necessarily synonymous with anthroposophy; our society is

---

1. At the time of this lecture, Rudolf Steiner was the leader of the Theosophical Society in Germany, much of which later became the Anthroposophical Society. Concerning that period, see *From the History & Contents of the First Section of the Esoteric School, 1904–1914* (see bibliography for this and all other citations).

not alone in cultivating esotericism, nor is this its only task. It may even be possible to join our society and avoid esotericism completely.

Among the pursuits of the Theosophical Society (in addition to the field of general ethics) is occult practice, which involves the laws of existence generally hidden from the sensory observation of everyday human experience. By no means, however, are these laws unrelated to everyday experience. *Occult* means "hidden" or "mysterious," but it must be emphasized again and again that esotericism necessarily involves preconditions. Higher mathematics would be incomprehensible to a simple peasant who had never encountered it; likewise, occult practice is incomprehensible to many people today. It ceases to be "occult," however, once one has mastered it. In this way, I have strictly defined the limits of today's lecture. Therefore—and this must be stressed in the light of the most manifold endeavors and the millennial experience—no one can argue that the requirements of esotericism are impossible or that they contradict culture in general. There is no expectation that anyone should fulfill such requirements, but those who ask for the assurances provided by esotericism while refusing to work with it are like a boy who wants to create electricity in a glass rod, yet refuses to rub it. Without friction, it cannot be charged. This is similar to the arguments against esoteric practice.

No one is urged to become an esotericist; people must come to esotericism of their own volition. Those who say that esotericism is unnecessary do not need to take it up. At the present time, occult practice does not appeal to humankind in general. Indeed, it is extremely difficult in today's culture to submit to the rules of conduct that will open the spirit world. Two prerequisites are completely absent in our culture. One is isolation— what spiritual science calls "higher human solitude"; the other is the matter of overcoming egoism, a dominant characteristic of our time, though largely unconscious. Without these two prerequisites, the path of inner development is simply unattainable. Isolation, or spiritual solitude, is very difficult to achieve, because life tends to distract and disperse people; it demands sensory involvement in the outer world. Never before has there been a culture in which people lived with such external involvement. Please do not take what I am saying as criticism; it is simply an objective description.

Of course, those who speak as I do know that the situation could not be otherwise, and that it is the basis for the greatest advantages and achievements of our day. But this is also the reason our time is so devoid of suprasensory discernment, and why our culture is so devoid of suprasensory influences. In other cultures (and they do exist), people are better able to cultivate the inner life and withdraw from outer influences. Such cultures offer a soil in which the higher inner life can thrive. In the cultures of the East one finds yoga, and those who live according to the rules of that teaching are called yogis. A yogi is one who strives for higher spiritual knowledge, but only after having worked to master the suprasensory world, and no one is able to proceed without the guidance of a master, or guru. Yogis who have found a guru must spend a considerable part of the day—regularly, not just occasionally—living totally within the soul. All the forces needed by a yogi for self-development are already within the soul. They exist there just as truly as electricity exists in a glass rod before it is evoked by friction. Evoking soul forces requires the methods of spiritual science, which are the results of observations over millennia. This is very difficult in life today, which requires a kind of splintering of individuals who struggle for existence. One cannot attain total inner composure; one cannot even attain the concept of such composure. People are not aware enough of the deep solitude that a yogi must seek. One must repeat the same material rhythmically and with immense regularity, if only for a brief time each day, completely separated from the usual concerns. All the life that usually surrounds the yogi must cease to exist and the senses must become unreceptive to surrounding worldly impressions. Yogis must be able to become deaf and mute to their surroundings during the time they prescribe for themselves. One must be able to concentrate to such a degree—and such concentration must be practiced—that a cannon could be fired nearby without disturbing the attention of one's inner life. One must also become free of all memory impressions, especially those of daily life.

There must be no hint of becoming estranged or distanced from ordinary practical life, otherwise one has strayed from the right course. If this happens, it may not be possible to distinguish one's higher life from insanity. It is, in fact, a kind of insanity when the inner life loses its normal relationship to the outer world. Imagine, for example, that you were knowledgeable about conditions on earth and that you had gained all the experience and wisdom that could be gathered here. One evening, you fall asleep, and in the morning you wake up not on Earth but on Mars. Conditions on Mars are completely different from those on Earth; the knowledge you gained on Earth is completely useless. There is no longer any harmony between your inner and outer life. Most likely, you would find yourself in a Martian insane asylum within an hour.

A similar situation might easily occur if inner development severs one's connection with the external world, and people must be very careful not to let this happen. These are great difficulties in our culture. Consider how very difficult it is to bring about these conditions in our culture—even the concept of this isolation is lacking. Spiritual solitude must be attained in such a

way that the harmony—the total equilibrium with the surrounding world—is never lost. But this harmony can be lost
quite easily during deep immersion in one's inner life. Those
who go more and more deeply inward must, at the same time,
be able to establish and increase their clarity and harmony with
the outer world.

In terms of inner soul qualities, egoism is the first obstacle.
People today usually ignore this. Egoism is closely connected
with human spiritual development. An important prerequisite
for spiritual development is that it not be sought out of egoism,
and those who are motivated by egoism will not get very far. But
egoism today reaches deeply into one's innermost soul. Again
and again, we hear the argument, "What is the use of all these
occult teachings if I cannot experience them for myself?" Those
who begin with this preconception and cannot change have little
chance of attaining higher development. One aspect of higher
development is an intimate awareness of human community, so
it makes no difference whether it is I or someone else who has
the experience. Hence, when I meet someone who is more
highly developed than I am, I must meet that person with
unlimited love and trust. First, I must acquire this consciousness, a consciousness of infinite trust toward my fellow human
beings, when they claim to have experienced one thing or
another. Such trust is needed to work together. Whenever occult
capacities are brought strongly into play, there is unlimited trust;
there is an awareness that this is someone in whom higher individuality lives. The primary foundation, therefore, is trust and
faith, because we do not seek the higher self only in ourselves
but also in others. Everyone around us lives in undivided unity
in the inner kernel of their being.

In terms of my lower self, I am separated from other people.
But as far as my higher self is concerned—and only this can

ascend to the spirit world—I am not separate from my fellow human beings but one with them, and those who speak to me from higher truths are in reality myself. I must avoid completely the notion of any difference between the other and me, and I must overcome totally any feeling that others have any advantage over me. Try to live with this feeling until it penetrates the most intimate fiber of your soul and causes every vestige of egoism to disappear. If you do this, someone further along the path will stand before you truly as yourself, and you will have attained one of the requirements for awakening higher spiritual life.

In some situations, esoteric guidance may be erroneous and confused. One may be told, for example, that the higher self already lives within us—simply let the inner I speak, and the highest truth will manifest. Nothing could be more correct and, at the same time, less productive than this assertion. Just try to let your inner I speak, and you will find that, as a rule, no matter how much you believe it is your higher self that manifests, it is really the lower self that speaks. This is because we cannot find the higher self within us yet, but must look for it outside ourselves. We can learn a great deal from one who is further along than we are, because the higher self is visible in such people. The higher I gains nothing from our egoistic self. Whereas someone may be further along than you are now, you will be there at some point in the future. You are truly constituted to carry within yourself the seed of what that person has become. The paths to Olympus, however, must first be illuminated before we can follow them.

There is a feeling that may seem incredible, but it is fundamental to all esoteric development. Various religions mention this, and every practicing esotericist will confirm it. Christianity describes it with the well-known sentence, which esotericists must understand completely: "Except ye ... become

as little children, ye shall not enter into the kingdom of heaven"
(Matt. 18:3). This can be understood only by those who have
learned the highest kind of reverence.

Suppose that, when you were very young, there was a venera-
ble person you held in the highest regard, and that you were
offered an opportunity to meet this individual. You feel a sense
of awe within as you approach, about to see this person for the
first time. There, standing at the doorway, you might feel hesi-
tant to touch the handle and open it. If you look up to a venera-
ble person in this way, you can begin to grasp what Christianity
means by saying that we must become as little children to enter
the kingdom of heaven. Whether the person is in fact worthy of
such veneration is unimportant; what matters is the capacity to
feel the veneration that arises from one's innermost heart. This
feeling of veneration is the elevating force, lifting us to higher
realms of suprasensory life. Those who seek the higher life must
write this occult law into their souls with golden letters. Development must begin with this fundamental soul mood; nothing
can be achieved without it.

Next, those seeking inner development must clearly understand that what they are doing is immensely important to the
human being. What they are looking for is no less than a new
birth, and this is meant literally; it is the birth of the higher
human soul. We were born from the deep inner foundations of
existence in our first birth, and emerged into the light of the sun;
similarly, those who seek inner development step from the light
of the physical sun into a higher spiritual light. It is the birth of
something that lies as deeply dormant in most human beings as
an unborn child does in the mother. Unless one understands the
full significance of this truth, esoteric development itself cannot
be understood. The higher soul, resting deep within human
nature and interwoven with it, is brought forth.

Higher and lower natures are integrated in those we encounter in ordinary life, and this is fortunate. Many among us would exhibit evil negative qualities, except that along with the lower nature there is a higher one that exerts a balancing influence. This intermixing may be compared to combining yellow and blue liquids in a glass, resulting in a green liquid in which blue and yellow can no longer be distinguished. Similarly, the lower human nature is mingled with the higher, and the two cannot be distinguished. However, you might extract the blue liquid from the green by a chemical process, so that only the yellow remains, with the green separated into a complete duality. Likewise, the lower and higher human natures separate through esoteric development. One draws the lower nature from the body like a sword from its scabbard, which then remains alone.

Lower human nature emerges and appears almost gruesome. While still mingled with the higher nature, nothing was noticeable, but once they separated, all evil negative qualities come into view. People who had always seemed benevolent often become argumentative and jealous. This characteristic existed earlier in the lower nature, but was guided by the higher. This can be observed in many of those who have been guided along an abnormal path. A person may become a liar when introduced to the spiritual realm, because the capacity to distinguish between the true and the false is easily lost. Therefore, a strict training of personal character must always go along with esoteric training. What history tells us about saints and their temptations is not legend but fact.

Those who wish to develop toward the higher world on any path are prone to temptations unless they can subdue everything they encounter with strong character and high morals. Not only do lust and passions grow—these are not generally the real problem—but opportunities also increase. It seems miraculous; as one ascends into higher worlds, previously hidden opportunities for evil lurk all around. In every area of life, a demon lies in wait, ready to lead us astray. We see now what we had not seen before, as through a spell, the division within our own being, conjures these opportunities from hidden areas of life. Consequently, a very determined formation of character is an indispensable basis for so-called white magic, the school of esoteric development that leads us into the higher worlds in a good, true, and genuine way. Any practicing esotericist will tell you that no one should dare to step through the "narrow portal" (as the entry to esoteric development is called) without practicing these qualities regularly; they form the necessary foundation for occult life.

First we must develop the ability to discern what is unimportant or important—that is, perishable or imperishable—in every situation in life. This requirement is easy to point out, but difficult to do. As Goethe said, it is easy, but the easy is difficult. Look, for example, at a plant or some object. You will be able to understand that everything has important and unimportant aspects, and that people are usually interested in what is unimportant, how it relates to themselves, or some lesser aspect. Those who wish to become esotericists must gradually develop the habit of looking for and seeing the essence of each thing. For instance, when we see a clock we must be interested in its principles. We must be able to disassemble it into the smallest parts and develop a feeling for the principles behind the clock. A mineralogist can gain considerable knowledge about a quartz crystal simply by looking at it. The esotericist, however, must be able to hold a stone and feel, in a living way, something like this: In a certain sense, this crystal is lower than humankind; but in a certain sense, it is also far above humankind. It is beneath humanity, because it cannot imagine a human being through concepts, nor can it feel. It cannot explain nor think nor even live, but it has one advantage over humankind. It is pure within itself, with no desire, no wishes, and no lust. Every human being—every living being—has wishes, desires, and lusts, which the crystal does not have. It is complete and without desire, satisfied with what comes to it—an example to humankind. We must unite this with our other qualities.

If esotericists can feel this in all its depth, then they have grasped what the stone has to say. Thus, we can draw something meaningful out of anything. Once this way of seeing has become a habit, we separate the important from the unimportant; we have acquired another essential feeling for esotericists. Then we must connect our life with what is important. Today, it is especially easy to make mistakes in this. People believe that their place in life is not appropriate; they are often inclined to say, Destiny has put me in the wrong place. I am (let's say) only a postal clerk. If I were in a different place, I could teach people great ideas—and so on. The mistake that such people make is that they never penetrate the significance of their occupation. If you see something important in me because I can talk to those who have gathered here, then you will not see the importance of your own life and work. If the mail carriers did not carry the mail, postal traffic would stop, and much of the work achieved by others would be in vain.

Every individual, wherever that person may be, is exceedingly important for the whole, and no one is higher than any other. Christ attempted to demonstrate this most beautifully in the Gospel of John, with these words: "The servant is not greater than his lord; neither he that is sent greater than he that sent him" (John 13:16). This was spoken after the master had washed the feet of the apostles. He wanted to say, "What would I be without my apostles? You must be here so that I can be here in the world, and I must pay you tribute by lowering myself to wash your feet." This is one of the most significant references to the esotericist's sense for what is important. What is important in the inner sense must not be confused with what is outwardly important. This must be strictly observed.

In addition, we must develop a series of qualities. To begin with, we must become masters over our thoughts, and particularly our train of thought. This is called control of thoughts.[2] Just consider the way thoughts whirl around in the human soul, fluttering about like a butterfly. An impression arises here, then another there, and each affects one's thoughts. It is not true that we are in charge of our thoughts; rather, our thoughts control us completely. We must gain the ability to steep ourselves in one specific thought at a certain time of the day, not allowing any other thought to enter and disturb the soul. In this way, we hold the reins of thought for awhile.

The second quality is similar, but in relation to our actions—that is, control of our actions. Here we need to do something, at least occasionally, that is not initiated externally. Nothing that is initiated by our place in life—one's profession or situation—leads us to higher life. The higher life depends on personal matters, such as the resolve to do something completely as a result of one's own initiative, even if that action is absolutely insignificant. No other action contributes anything to the higher life.

The third quality to work for is equanimity. People fluctuate back and forth between joy and sorrow, one moment filled with joy, the next unbearably sad. Thus people allow themselves to be rocked on the waves of life, joy and sorrow. But we must reach equanimity and steadiness. Neither the greatest sorrow nor the greatest joy must unsettle one's composure. We must become steadfast and even-tempered.

---

2. For more on these exercises, see *An Outline of Esoteric Science*, chapter 5.

Fourth is an understanding of every being. Nothing expresses this more beautifully than a legend handed down to us by a Persian story rather than by a Gospel. Jesus was walking over a field with his disciples, and on the way they found a decaying dog's body. The animal looked horrible. Jesus stopped and gave it an admiring look, saying, "What beautiful teeth this animal has!" Jesus found one beautiful quality in something ugly. Always try to find what is wonderful in every aspect of outer reality, and you will see that everything contains something positive. Do as Christ did when he admired the beautiful teeth on the dead dog. This path will lead you to tremendous tolerance and to an understanding of every being and thing.

The fifth quality is complete openness toward everything new that we encounter. Most people judge new things according to what they already know. When someone tells them something new, they immediately respond with an opposing opinion. But we must never confront new communication by immediately giving our own opinion. Rather, we must always be on the lookout for the possibility of learning something new; we can learn even from a small child. The wisest person must be willing to withhold judgment and to listen to others. We must develop the ability to listen, for it enables us to meet events with the greatest possible openness. This is called faith in esotericism. This is the ability to refrain from opposing the new, which weakens its impression.

The sixth quality is something we all gain once we have developed the first five: inner harmony. Those who have the other qualities become inwardly harmonious. In addition, it is necessary for a person seeking esoteric development to develop a feeling for freedom to the highest degree. That sense of freedom enables us to seek within ourselves the center of our own being and to stand on our own two feet. Thus, we do not have to ask everyone what to do, but can stand upright and act freely. This is another quality that we need to acquire.

Those who have developed these inner qualities stand above all the dangers that arise from the division of their nature. As a result, the qualities of one's lower nature no longer have any effect, and one can no longer stray from the path. These qualities must be formed with the greatest precision. The occult life follows, and its expression requires that one carry a steady rhythm into life. To "carry a steady rhythm into life" means the development of this faculty. If you observe nature, you find there a certain rhythm. You expect, of course, that the violet will bloom every year at the same time in spring, and that the crops in the field and the grapes on the vine will ripen around the same time each year. This rhythmic sequence of phenomena exists everywhere in nature. Everywhere there is rhythm, everywhere repetition in regular sequence. As you ascend from plants to higher beings, you see this rhythmic sequence decrease. Yet even in the higher stages of animal development, one sees that functions are ordered rhythmically. At a certain time of the year, animals acquire certain functions and capacities. As beings evolve to higher levels, life is given more into the hands of those beings themselves, and rhythms decrease. You must know that the physical body is only one member of the human being. There are also an ether body, an astral body, and the higher members, which form the foundation for the others.

The physical body is highly subject to the rhythm that governs outer nature. The life of the physical body takes its course rhythmically, just as plant and animal life does in its external form. The heart beats in a rhythm, the lungs breathe in a rhythm, and so on. All of this moves along rhythmically, because its order was set by higher powers, the wisdom of the world, or what the scriptures call Holy Spirit. The higher bodies (especially the astral body) have been abandoned by these higher spiritual forces, as it were, and lost their rhythm. Can you deny that your activities related to wishes, desires, and passions are irregular—that they can never be compared to the regularity of the physical body? Those who have come to understand the inherent rhythm of physical nature find an example for spirituality in it. Consider the heart, for example, this wonderful organ with a regular beat and innate wisdom, and then compare it with the desires and passions that arise from the astral body and unleash all sorts of acts against the heart. You can see how its normal course is harmed by passion. The functions of the astral body, however, must become as rhythmic as those of the physical body.

More than ever, it is necessary for people today to carry rhythm into every area of higher life. God implanted rhythm in our physical body, and we must give our astral body rhythm; we must order our daily lives. People must arrange life for the astral body, just as the spirit of nature arranges life for the lower realms. In the morning, at a specific time, one must perform one spiritual act; another must be done regularly at another time of day, and yet another in the evening. These spiritual exercises must not be chosen arbitrarily, but be suited to the development of higher life. This is one method for taking charge of life and keeping it that way. Set a time for yourself in the morning when you will concentrate, and then adhere that time. You must establish a kind of calm, so that your inner occult master may be awakened.

You must meditate on a great thought that has nothing to do with the outer world. Let this thought come to life completely. A short time is enough, perhaps fifteen minutes. Even five minutes are sufficient, if that's all you have available. It is worthless to do these exercises, however, if they are not done regularly. Do them consistently so that the astral body's activity becomes as regular as a clock; only then will they have any value. The astral body will seem completely different if you do these exercises on a regular basis. If you sit in the morning and do these exercises, the forces I have described will develop. But, as I said, it must be done regularly, for the astral body expects that the same process will take place at the same time each day, and it becomes disordered if this does not happen. There must at least be an intent toward order. If you make your life rhythmic in this way, it will not be long before you see success; the spirit life that has been hidden from humankind for the time being will manifest to a certain degree.

I want to mention something here that will seem like an exaggeration to most people; this is the matter of fasting. People have completely lost any awareness of the significance of fasting. It is enormously important, however, for creating rhythm in our astral body. What does it mean to fast? It means that we restrain the desire to eat and block the astral body's desire in relation to this. Those who fast block the astral body and suppress the desire to eat. It is like blocking a machine's force. The astral body becomes inactive, and the whole rhythm of the physical body and its innate wisdom works upward into the astral body, making it rhythmic. Like the imprint of a seal, the harmony of the physical body impresses itself upon the astral body. This would transfer much more permanently if the astral body did not always become irregular because of desires, passions, and wishes—including spiritual desires and wishes.

In general, human life alternates among four states. The first is our perception of the outer world. You look around with your senses and perceive the external world. The second is what we may call imagination, or the life of mental images, which is related to, even part of, our dream life. Here, people are not rooted in their surroundings but separate from them; people have no realities within themselves but, at best, only memories.

The third state is dreamless sleep, in which people are completely unaware of their I. In the fourth state, people live in memory. This is not like perception but something remote, or spiritual. If we had no memory, we would be unable to uphold any spiritual development.

The inner life begins to develop through inner contemplation and meditation. Sooner or later, one perceives that dreams no longer occur in a chaotic way; one begins to dream in the most meaningful way, and remarkable things reveal themselves through dreams, which one gradually begins to recognize as manifestations of spirit beings. Of course, one can raise the trivial argument that this is merely a dream and thus inconsequential. If, however, an airship is revealed in a dream and then one builds it, we can see that the dream simply showed the truth. Thus an idea can be grasped by unusual means. Its truth must then be judged by whether it can be realized. We are convinced of its inner truth by its outer expression.

The next step in spiritual life is to apprehend truth by means of our own qualities and by consciously guiding our dreams. When we begin to guide our dreams in a regular way, we have reached the stage at which truth becomes transparent for us. The first stage is called "material cognition," for which the object must appear before us. The next stage is "imaginative cognition." This is developed by meditation, by forming one's life rhythmically. It is a laborious process, but once it is achieved, the time comes when there is no longer any difference between the perception of ordinary life and that of the suprasensory world. While among the phenomena of ordinary life in the sensory world, we can change our spiritual state and continuously experience the spiritual, suprasensory world—but only if we have trained ourselves sufficiently. This happens once we are able to become deaf and dumb to the sensory world and forget everyday life, while retaining an inner spiritual life. Our dream life then begins to assume a conscious form.

If we are able to pour some of this into daily life, the next capacity arises, making the soul qualities of beings around us perceptible. We begin to see not only the outer aspect of things, but also the inner, hidden essence of things—that of plants, animals, and other people. I know that most people will say that these are in fact different things. True, these things are always different from what a person sees without such senses. This third stage is one in which a particular consciousness—one that is usually completely empty—begins to be enlivened by continual awareness. This continuity appears on its own. One is then no longer unconscious while asleep. During the time one used to be asleep, one now experiences the spirit world.

What is the nature of ordinary sleep? The physical body lies in bed, and the astral body lives in the suprasensory world; you "go for a walk" in the suprasensory realm. As a rule, the disposition of most people today prevents them from going very far from the physical body. We know that, by applying the principles of spiritual science, we can develop organs in the astral body for its wanderings during sleep—just as the physical body has organs—and that they allow one to be conscious while asleep. Without eyes and ears, the physical body would be blind and deaf, and for the same reason the astral body is blind and deaf in its nightly walk, because it still lacks "eyes and ears." One can develop these organs, however, through meditation, which is the means for training such organs. Such meditation must be guided in a regular way. It is led in such a way that the human body is the mother and the human spirit is the father.

The physical human body, as we see it before us, is a mystery in each of its parts—indeed, each member is related in a specific (though mysterious) way to an aspect of the astral body. These are matters an esotericist knows. For instance, the point in the physical body between the eyebrows is connected with a certain organ in the astral organism. Esotericism indicates that we must direct our thoughts, feelings, and sensations to a point between the eyebrows by connecting something formed in the physical body with the corresponding aspect of the astral body, which leads to a certain sensation in the astral body. This must be practiced regularly, and one must know how it is done. In this way, the astral body begins to form its members. It grows from a shapeless mass into an organism in which organs have formed. I have described the astral sense organs in the magazine *Lucifer Gnosis*.[3] These are also called "lotus flowers" and are cultivated by means of special word sequences. Once this has been done, one is able to perceive the spirit world—the same world we enter when we pass through the portal of death and a final contradiction to Hamlet's "undiscovered country from whose bourn no traveller returns."

Thus it is possible to go, or rather "slip," from the sensory world into the suprasensory one and to live in both at once. This does not imply that one lives in a never-never land, but in a world that clarifies and explains our own. An ordinary person who has never studied electricity would not understand all the wonderful functions in an electrically powered factory; similarly, the average person does not understand the events of the spirit world. As long as one remains ignorant of electrical principles, one will also fail to understand what goes on in a factory. Likewise, one will lack understanding in the realm of the spirit as long as there is no understanding of spiritual principles. There is

---

3. Rudolf Steiner edited this periodical, in which he first published a number of articles that eventually became his books *The Stages of Higher Knowledge* and *How to Know Higher Worlds;* see especially pages 112–117 regarding the development of the human astral centers called "lotus flowers."

nothing in our world that does not depend on the spirit world every moment. Everything around us is the outer expression of the spirit world. Materiality does not exist; everything material is, in fact, condensed spirit. For those who can look into the spirit world, the entire material sensory world—the world in general—becomes spiritualized. Everything sensory melts into something spiritual within the souls of those who see into the spirit world, just as the warmth of the sun causes ice to melt into water. Thus, the ground of the world gradually manifests to one's spiritual eyes and ears.

The life that we come to know in this way is, in reality, the spiritual life we have carried within ourselves all along. But we knew nothing of it, because we did not know ourselves before we developed organs for perceiving the higher world. Imagine having all the characteristics you have now, but without any sensory organs. You would have no knowledge of the world around you and no understanding of the physical body, yet you would nevertheless be part of the physical world. Similarly, the human soul belongs to the spirit world, but the soul does not know this because it does not hear or see. Just as our body is drawn from the forces and materials of the physical world, our soul is drawn from the forces and materials of the spirit world. We do not recognize ourselves within ourselves, but only within our surroundings. One cannot perceive an organ such as a heart or a brain, even by x-ray, without seeing it in others through our sense organs; only the eyes can see the heart. Likewise, we cannot truly see or hear our own soul without perceiving it with spiritual organs in the surrounding world. You recognize yourself only in relation to your surroundings. In truth, there is no inner knowledge, no self-examination; there is only one kind of knowledge, or revelation; it is our knowledge of life around us through both the physical and the spiritual organs. We are a part of the worlds around us—the physical, the soul, and the spirit. If we have physical organs, we learn from the physical; if we have spiritual and soul organs, we learn from the spirit world and from every soul. There is no knowledge except knowledge of the world.

It is vain and useless to "brood" within yourself, thinking it is possible to progress simply by looking within. You will find the god within yourself by awaking your inner divine organs and finding your higher divine self all around you, just as you find your lower self by simply using your eyes and ears. We perceive ourselves clearly as physical beings by interacting with the sensory world, and we perceive ourselves clearly in the spirit world by developing spiritual senses. Inner development means opening yourself to the divine life all around you.

Now you will understand why it is so essential for those who rise to the higher world to begin with an immense strengthening of character. One can naturally experience the characteristics of the sensory world, because those senses are already open. This is possible because a benevolent divine spirit—one who saw and heard in the physical world—stood by humankind during the most ancient times, before any ability to see and hear, and opened human eyes and ears. It is from these very beings that people must now learn to see spiritually. They are beings who can already do what people have yet to learn. We need a guru who can tell us how to develop our organs, one who will tell us how these organs have already been developed in others. Those who wish to guide must have one fundamental quality: unconditional honesty. This quality is also a fundamental requirement for the student. No one may train to become an esotericist unless this fundamental quality of unconditional honesty has been cultivated.

When dealing with sensory experience, we can verify what we are told. When I tell you about the spirit world, however, you must trust, because you haven't gone far enough to confirm that information. Those who would like to become gurus must be so honest that it is impossible to take lightly any statement about the spirit world or spiritual life. By its very nature, the sensory world corrects errors immediately; in the spirit world, we need inner guidelines. We must be strictly trained, so that we do not need the outer world as controls, but only our inner self. We can gain such control only by acquiring, within this world, the strictest honesty. Consequently, when the Theosophical Society began to present the world with some of the fundamental esoteric teachings, it had to adopt the principle that there is no law higher than truth, but very few understand this principle.

People are generally satisfied with being able to say they are convinced that something is true, and if it turns out to be wrong, they simply say that they were mistaken. Esotericists cannot rely on this kind of subjective honesty; it is on the wrong path. They must always remain in harmony with the facts of the external world, and if any experience contradicts those facts, it must be seen as an error. The question of who is to blame for an error is no longer important to esotericists. They must be in absolute agreement with the facts in life, and they must begin to feel a strict responsibility for everything they assert. Consequently, esotericists train themselves in the unconditional certainty they need, both for themselves and for others, if they wish to be spiritual guides.

So you see that I needed to point out a series of qualities and methods. We need to discuss these again and add the higher concepts. You may feel that these matters are too intimate for discussion and that each soul must come to terms with them individually. You may feel that they are not suited to reaching the great destination—entry to the spirit world—but this will certainly be accomplished by those who take the path I described. When will this happen? One of the most outstanding participants in the theosophical movement, Subba Row (who died some time ago), spoke appropriately of this.[4] Answering this question of how long it takes, he said, "Seven years, perhaps also seven times seven years, perhaps even seven incarnations, perhaps only seven hours." It all depends on what we bring with us into life. We may meet someone who seems very stupid but brought into life a concealed higher life that merely needs to be brought out. Most people today are much more advanced than they seem, and more people would know this if the materialistic conditions of our time did not drive them back into their inner life of the soul.

A great many people today were previously much more advanced. Whether their inner qualities will emerge depends on many factors, but it is possible to help. Suppose you are faced with a person who was highly developed in an earlier incarnation, but whose brain is now undeveloped. Undeveloped brain capacity may sometimes conceal great spiritual faculties. But if one can be taught ordinary everyday abilities, such a person's inner spirituality may also emerge.

Another important factor is one's environment. Human beings are mirror images of their surroundings in a very important sense. Imagine someone who is a highly developed but lives in an environment that awakens and develops such strong preconceptions that the higher talents cannot emerge. Unless someone can draw out those abilities, they will remain hidden.

I have been able to present only a few indications about this subject. After Christmas, however, we will speak again about more advanced and deeper matters. I especially wanted to arouse

---

4. T. Subba Row (1856–1890), an attorney in Madras, India, who was a Theosophist and colleague of H.P. Blavatsky.

in you the understanding that the higher life is not trained in a chaotic way, but very intimately in the deepest soul. In truth, that great day—when the soul awakens and enters the higher life—comes like the thief in the night. Development toward the higher life leads us into a new world, and when we have entered that new world, we see "the other side of existence." Then, what has previously been hidden reveals itself. You might say to yourself that perhaps not everyone can do this, but only a few. However, that must not keep you from at least beginning on the path that is open to everyone—that is, to hear about the higher worlds. People are called to live in community, and those who seclude themselves cannot attain the spiritual life. But one becomes even more secluded by saying, "I don't believe this; it has nothing to do with me. Maybe it makes sense for the afterlife." For esotericists, this has no truth. An important principle for esotericists is to consider others to be true manifestations of their own higher self, because they know then that they must find the others within themselves. There is a delicate distinction between these two phrases—"to find others in oneself" and "to find oneself in others." In the higher sense it means, "You are that" [*tat tsvam asi*]. And in the highest sense, it means to recognize yourself in the world and to understand that saying of the poet I cited some time ago in a different context: "One was successful. He lifted the veil of the goddess at Sais. But what did he see? Miracle of miracles! He saw himself." To find oneself—not in egoistic inwardness, but selflessly in the outer world—that is true self-knowledge.

2. The Psychological Basis of Spiritual Science

I would like to discuss the scientific nature and value of a spiritual trend that most people would hesitate to call "scientific" at all. This spiritual movement is called theosophy (an allusion to various similar endeavors today). In the history of philosophy, this name has been applied to certain spiritual movements that emerged repeatedly during the history of human culture. This discussion, however, is unrelated to those, though it does contain many reminders of them. Consequently, we will limit ourselves to what may be described here as a special condition of the mind, and we will disregard opinions about what is typically called theosophy. If we adhere to this perspective, it will be possible to say precisely how we might view the relationship between the spiritual movement we have in mind and the views that define contemporary science and philosophy.

Let us admit without reservation that, even in terms of the *concept* of knowledge, it is difficult to find a relationship between so-called theosophy and any seemingly well established notions of "science" and "fact"—which have and will certainly continue to bring such great benefits to human society. The past few centuries have led to the practice of using the word *scientific* to describe only those matters that can be readily verified by anyone at any time through observation, experiment, and elaboration through human intellect. "Science" eliminates as unverifiable anything that is limited to subjective significance in the human mind.

It can hardly be denied that the philosophical concept of knowledge has for quite some time adapted itself to the scientific view I just described. We see this especially in today's investigations related to what may be allowed as an object of human knowledge, as well as the point where this knowledge must acknowledge its limits. It would be superfluous for me to support this statement with an outline of contemporary research in epistemology. I would like to emphasize only the goal of such research, in which it is presumed that the relationship between human beings and the outer world offers a determinable idea of the cognitive process, and that this concept of knowledge provides a basis for describing all that lies within the reach of cognition. Regardless of how greatly theoretical trends may diverge from one another, if this description is taken in a broad enough sense, you can find there a common thread in the decisive philosophical movements.

The concept of knowledge belonging to what we call spiritual science seems to contradict the ideas just described. In its view, knowledge cannot be deduced directly by looking at human nature and its relationship to the external world. Based on the established facts concerning thought processes, spiritual science considers it reasonable to say that knowledge is not "finished" and complete as such, but is fluid and able to evolve. It believes it is correct to say that, the human being can penetrate beyond the horizon of normal consciousness. It needs to be emphasized that the mental life we are talking about here should not be thought of as the so-called subconscious. The subconscious can be studied by science using common research methods; it can be made the object of inquiry, just like any other natural or mental phenomena. But that has nothing to do with the state of the mind we are speaking of, in which we are completely conscious and are complete self-aware, just as one is in ordinary consciousness. This state of mind must first be created by means of certain exercises and soul experiences; it cannot be assumed as a given in human nature. This mental state represents a development of the human mind—of presence of mind and other signs of conscious mental life as such development continues.

I wish to describe this state of mind and show how its fruits may be classified according to modern scientific epistemology. My purpose is thus to describe the method used by this spiritual movement, based on a potential development of the mind. The first part of my exposition may be called a spiritual-scientific way of viewing things based on certain psychologically possible facts. My descriptions should be regarded as mental experiences that may come to awareness once certain prerequisites have been achieved in the mind. The epistemological value of these experiences will not be assessed until they have been described briefly.

The activity to be performed may be called a mental exercise. The first step is to consider, from a different point of view, mental contents normally evaluated according to their likeness to an external phenomenon. In the concepts and ideas we form, first we want to have a copy, or token, of something that exists outside those concepts. Spiritual researchers, in this sense, look for mental contents similar to the concepts of ordinary life or scientific research. We do not, however, compare their cognitional value to the object, but allow them to exist in the mind as operative forces. We plant them as spiritual seeds, so to speak, in the soil of the mind's life, and wait with a completely serene spirit for their effect on this mental life.

Thus we can observe that, by repeating such an exercise, our state of mind changes. It must be emphasized, however, that what really counts is *repetition*. The important thing is not that the concepts' ordinary meaning should affect the mind as a way of knowledge. On the contrary, we are concerned with an actual process of the mind's life itself. In this process, concepts do not act as cognitional elements, but as real *forces;* their effect depends on those same forces that frequently take hold of the mind's life. The effect achieved in the mind depends mostly on this require-ment: the same force must repeatedly take hold of the experience related to the concept. Consequently, we gain the best results by repeatedly meditating on the same content at specific intervals over relatively long periods of time.

The duration of our meditation is not very important in this case. It may be very brief, as long as it is accompanied by abso-lute serenity of soul, and as long as the mind eliminates all exter-nal sensory impressions and normal intellectual activity. The essential thing is that the mind is isolated with the content. This needs to be mentioned, because it must be clearly understood that the practice of these mental exercises does not need to create a disturbance in anyone's normal life. As a rule, the time needed is available to everyone. And if the exercises are done correctly, the change they produce in the mind does not make the slightest difference in the consciousness needed for the normal human life. Even if undesirable excesses and peculiarities occur because of one's particular predisposition, this should not in any way alter one's judgment of the essential nature of the practice.

For this mental discipline, the ordinary concepts of human life are useless for the most part. Mental topics that relate mostly to objective elements outside themselves are for the most part ineffective when used for the exercises described. Mental pic-tures are far more suitable if they are symbolic in nature. The most fruitful of all are those that encompass a lively connection to multiple meanings. Consider this example, proven by experi-ence to be beneficial: Goethe's idea of the archetypal plant. One may mention the fact that, in a conversation with Schiller, Goethe drew a brief, symbolic image of this archetypal plant. He said that, if one can bring this picture to life in the mind, it would be possible to create from this (by modifying it according to law) every possible form of plant. Whatever one may think of the objective cognitional value of such a symbolic archetypal plant, if it is brought to life in the mind as indicated, and if one waits for its effects on the mind in serenity, something happens that could be considered a changed constitution of mind.

The mental images that spiritual scientists claim to be useful in this way may occasionally seem strange, but this sense of strangeness can be eliminated by understanding that such images should not be considered for their value as facts in an ordinary sense; they should be seen in terms of their effectiveness as real forces in the mind. A spiritual scientist does not attribute value to the meaning of the images used for mental exercises, but to the mind's experience of their influence.

Of course, one can give only a few examples of effective symbolic images. For example, imagine the human being so that the lower human nature (related to the animal organism) appears as a spirit being in relation to the human. This is done by symbolically uniting an animal shape with the highest ideal human form superimposed upon it—say, something like a centaur. The more alive the symbol appears as an image and the more saturated with meaning, the better it is. Under these conditions, the symbol affects the mind so that, after a certain time (of course, somewhat long), the inner life processes themselves are felt to be stronger, more flexible, and mutually illuminating.

An old symbol that may be used with good results is the so-called staff of Mercury—the mental image of a straight line, around which a spiral curves. Naturally, one must imagine this figure to be symbolic of a force system, so that, for example, one force system runs along the straight line, with another of lower velocity passing through the spiral. Expressed concretely, in connection with this figure, one may imagine the growth of a plant's stem with leaves sprouting along its length. One may also imagine it as an electromagnet. Furthermore, a picture of a human being's development may arise, with the enhancing capacities represented by the straight line, and the manifold impressions corresponding to the path of the spiral.

Mathematical forms may be especially meaningful, to the extent that symbols of cosmic processes can be seen in them. A good example is the so-called Cassini curve, with its three figures: the form resembling an ellipse, the lemniscate, and the two corresponding branches. Here the important thing is to experience the mental image so that the appropriate mental impressions accompany the transition of one curve into the other according to mathematical principles.

Other exercises may then be added to these. They also involve symbols, but these correspond to images expressed verbally. For example, with the symbol of light consider the wisdom that may be imagined as living and weaving in the orderly processes of cosmic phenomena. Wisdom expressed as sacrificial love may be thought of as the warmth that arises in the presence of light. One may think of sentences that are only symbolic of such concepts; the mind can be absorbed in meditation on such sentences. Essentially, the result depends on the degree of serenity and solitude of soul within the symbol during meditation. Success comes when the soul feels as though lifted out of the physical organism; it experiences a change in its sense of existence.

In normal life, we have the sense that our conscious life, arising from a unity, assumes a specific character according to the thoughts we derive from the percepts of individual senses. The result of these exercises, however, is that the mind feels imbued by an experience of itself. This is not as sharply differentiated in transition from one aspect of experience to another as, say, color and tone representations are within the limits of ordinary consciousness. The mind has the experience that it can withdraw to an area of inner being gained from the success of these exercises, one that was empty and could not be perceived before these exercises were practiced.

Many transitional stages occur in one's state of mind before such an inner experience is reached. One stage manifests as attentive observation (to be acquired through the exercise) of the moment when awaking from sleep. It is possible at these times to clearly sense how, out of something previously unknown, forces systematically take hold of the physical body's structure. As if the memory of something is arising, one feels the effects of this "thing" that has been working on the physical organization during sleep. If we have also acquired the capacity to experience this thing within our physical organization, we will clearly perceive the difference between the way this thing relates to the body while awake and asleep. We must say, then, that while we are awake this thing is within the body and while asleep it is outside. We must not, however, associate this "inside" and "outside" with ordinary spatial notions, but simply use these terms to describe experiences specific to a mind that has practiced the exercises described.

These exercises have an intimate soul character and take a unique form in each person. Once we have begun, the element of individuality results from the way each soul is used in practicing the exercises. What always follows, however, is a positive awareness of living in a reality that is suprasensory in nature and independent of one's outer physical body. For the sake of simplicity, let us refer to one who is looking for these soul experiences as a "spiritual researcher." For a spiritual researcher there is a definite awareness, in complete presence of mind, that behind the bodily organization perceptible to the senses there is a supra-sensory organization. There is an awareness that it is possible to experience oneself within this suprasensory organization just as normal consciousness is aware of itself within the physical body.[1]

By continuing these exercises in the right way, the "thing" described turns into a kind of spiritually organized state. One's consciousness becomes aware that its relationship to the supra-sensory world is similar to its connection to the sensory world through the senses. It is quite natural that one immediately begins to doubt the reality of this knowing relationship between the suprasensory aspect of the human being and the surrounding world. There may be a tendency to consider everything one experiences this way to be illusion, hallucination, suggestion, and so on. It is impossible to dismiss such doubt using theoretical arguments. Theories concerning the existence of a suprasensory world have no place here; it is a matter of possible experiences and observations presented to one's consciousness, exactly as observations are mediated by one's external sense organs.

Consequently, for one's experience of the suprasensory world, the only kind of recognition needed is the one a person also employs in the world of color, sound, and so on. Yet we must recognize that, when these exercises are practiced correctly—and, most important, with continued presence of mind—spiritual researchers can discern through direct observation the difference between an imaginary suprasensory world and one that is actually experienced, just as one can discern the difference in the sensory world between imagining the touch of a hot iron and actually touching it. Through practicing the exercises, spiritual

---

1. The exercises described are mentioned only in principle here. A detailed presentation may be found in *How to Know Higher Worlds*. — RUDOLF STEINER

researchers gain more and more certainty related specifically to the differences among hallucination, illusion, and suprasensory reality. Of course, careful spiritual researchers must be extremely critical of their own suprasensory observations. They always speak of their positive results of suprasensory research with reservation; something has been observed, and one's critical caution assumes that the same observations will be made by anyone who has established a relationship with the suprasensory world through the appropriate exercises. Differences among the statements of individual spiritual researchers must be seen as one would the descriptions of various travelers who have visited the same place but speak of it differently.

In *How to Know Higher Worlds*, the world described as above the horizon of consciousness is called (in keeping with those who have been spiritual researchers in this area) the *imaginative world*. You must not associate this expression, used in a purely technical sense, with anything that suggests a world created by mere fantasy. *Imaginative* is intended merely to suggest a qualitative character of the mind's content. This resembles the imaginations of ordinary consciousness, except that an imagination in the physical world is not directly related to anything real, whereas the imaginations of a spiritual researcher can be unmistakably ascribed to a suprasensory phenomenon, just as one's mental image of a color in the sensory world can be ascribed to an objective reality.

The life and movement in the soul made possible in this way can be called true self-awareness. One's inner being thus comes to self-knowledge, but not merely through self-regard as the bearer of sensory impressions or as an interpreter of those impressions through thinking. On the contrary, one's soul sees itself as it is, without a relationship to anything coming from the senses; it experiences itself "in itself," as a suprasensory reality.

This experience is not like that of the I in ordinary self-reflection—when attention is withdrawn from what it recognizes in the environment and, instead, is directed back to the knowing self. In that activity, consciousness "shrinks" to the point of one's I-being. This is not what happens as real self-knowledge arises in a spiritual researcher, in whom the soul becomes continuously richer with practice. One lives within lawful interrelationships; one's self does not experience itself outside the web of laws, as one does the laws of nature, which are taken from outer, worldly phenomena. On the contrary, it is aware of being within that web and united with its laws.

Knowledge of the *imaginative* world, however, is only the first step in spiritual research, and little more can be learned there about the suprasensory world, other than its outer aspect. Another step is needed. This requires deepening one's soul life— deeper than what was considered in the first step. Intense concentration on one's soul life, brought about by the exercises, enables a spiritual researcher to completely eliminate the meaning of symbols from awareness. In consciousness, one holds on to only the process through which the inner life went while absorbed in the symbols. The meaning of the symbols must be thrown away as a kind of abstraction, and only the *form of the experience* of those symbols must remain. The abstract meaning of the formed mental images—which was significant only during the transitional stage of soul development—is thus eliminated, and one's object of meditation becomes the inner weaving of the mind itself. Any description of this process is like a feeble shadow compared to the actual experience. What seems to be a simple description, in fact, derives its very meaning from the force of soul one exerts.

The danger that may arise at this stage of practice does so because one may believe prematurely—through a lack of real presence of mind—that the final result has been attained, and that the mere aftereffects of the symbolic inner pictures are the inner life itself. But this inner life is obviously without value, and must not be mistaken for the inner life that appears at the right time and announces itself to true circumspection. Although it manifests complete reality, it is nevertheless unlike any previous experience of reality.

Now it becomes possible to add suprasensory knowledge having a greater certainty than that of mere imaginative cognition. At this point in the soul's development, it may happen that one's inner experience is gradually filled with meaning that enters the mind similar to the way interpretations of sensory perception enter through the senses from the outer world. However, one fills the mind with suprasensory meaning by actually living within that meaning. To use an example from ordinary life, we can say that, when the I unites with spiritual meaning, it is similar to what one might experience when the I unites with a remembered image. Yet there is a distinction: the essence of what one unites with cannot in any way be compared to anything previously experienced; it is not related to anything in the past, but only to the present. Knowledge of this kind may be called knowledge through *inspiration,* as long as this term is associated only with what we've described. I have used the word as a technical term in *How to Know Higher Worlds.*[2]

In connection with this "knowing through inspiration," a new experience appears. In other words, the way one becomes aware of the mind's essence is entirely subjective; it does not initially manifest as objective. One recognizes it as something experienced, but does not have a sense of confronting it. This arises

---

2. See also, Rudolf Steiner, *A Psychology of Body, Soul, and Spirit,* "*Imagination*–Imagination; *Inspiration*–Self-Fulfillment; *Intuition*–Conscience," pp. 188ff.

only after one has condensed it within itself, so to speak, through soul energy. Only in this way does it become something we can view objectively. In this soul process, however, one becomes aware that there is still another entity between the physical organization and this "something" that has been separated off by the exercises. If we want to name these things, we can use terms that have become customary in so-called theosophy—provided we don't connect all sorts of fantastic notions with these terms and use them only as described. That "something" in which the self lives, as though in a being free of the bodily organization, is called an "astral body." What we discover between the astral body and the physical organism is called an "ether body."[3]

It is this ether body that provides the forces that enable the self to objectively perceive subjective, inspired knowledge. And one may ask with good reason how a spiritual researcher comes to the point of attributing such perception to a suprasensory world rather than one's own creation. No one would have any right to do this, except that the ether body (which we experience in relation to soul process) conforms to an inner law that compels us to do so objectively. And this is how it works, because we experience the ether body as a confluence of the all-encompassing complex of macrocosmic principles. It is not important how much of this complex enters a spiritual researcher's awareness. The strange fact is that direct cognition clearly sees that the ether body is simply a compacted image of the cosmic web of laws. Initially, a spiritual researcher's knowledge of the ether body does not go far enough to show what aspects of the universal, cosmic web of laws this formation reflects, but only the content of that formation.

And there are other reasonable doubts that ordinary consciousness may entertain concerning spiritual research. One may

---

3. One must not associate this with the "ether" of physics. — RUDOLF STEINER.

note the findings of such research (as related by contemporary literature) and say, "On closer scrutiny, what you describe as suprasensory knowledge is really nothing but combinations of ordinary views taken from the sensory world." And, in fact, people do say this.[4]

Countering this view, however, it must be said that, when spiritual researchers wish to express their experiences, they are required to use the means available to sensory thinking for expressing experiences in a suprasensory world. The experience must not be thought of as identical to the means of expression; rather, the means of expression is merely like the words of a language one must use. One must not look for the essence of such experiences in the mode of expression or in various illustrative images, but in the way these expressions are used. The difference between one's presentation and a fantastic accumulation of sensory images lies in the fact that a fantasy arises from arbitrary subjectivity, whereas any presentation by a spiritual researcher is based on a conscious familiarity with the suprasensory complex of laws, which is acquired through practice.

This is also the reason why the presentations of spiritual researchers can be so easily misunderstood; *how* one speaks is more important than what one says. This "how" reflects the suprasensory experience. If it is argued that what the spiritual researcher says, then, is not related directly to the ordinary world, it must be emphasized that the means of the presentation does, in fact, meet the practical requirements for an explanation of the sensory world drawn from a suprasensory sphere, and that

---

4. Likewise, my descriptions of the higher worlds that I felt appropriate to present in *Theosophy* and *An Outline of Esoteric Science* are found to be, so it seems, simply combinations of ideas taken from the sense world—as, for example, my descriptions of earth's evolution through combinations of entities of warmth, light, and so on. — RUDOLF STEINER

one's understanding of the world process perceptible to the senses is helped by real attention to the discoveries of the spiritual researcher.

Another skeptic may ask what a spiritual researcher's assertions have to do with the content of ordinary consciousness, since it can be said that this consciousness cannot test those findings. This last statement is, in principle, especially false. Research carried out to discover the facts of the suprasensory world requires a state of mind arises only as a result of the practices described. This, however, does not apply to testing it. When the discoveries of a spiritual researcher are communicated, if it is the truth, ordinary, open-minded logic is enough to know, in principle, that the world and life presented to the senses become understandable. One's initial opinion of a spiritual researcher's experiences is unimportant; they may be seen as hypotheses or regulative principles (in the Kantian sense). If one simply applies them to the sensory world, it can be seen, with time, that the sensory world confirms everything stated by the spiritual researcher. Of course, this applies only in principle; obviously, in their details, the assertions of so-called spiritual researchers may contain grave errors.

And there is another experience of spiritual research that will not happen unless the exercises are taken still further. Such progress means that, after attaining self-awareness, a spiritual researcher will be able to suppress this experience through an energetic force of volition. One must be able to free the mind from everything that has been attained through the continued effects of the exercises based on the outer sensory world. Symbolic images are formed from sensory images. The inner life and movement of the self in relation to inspired knowing is certainly free of the symbols themselves, yet it is still the result of exercises carried out under their influence. Although inspired knowledge brings a direct relationship between the self and the suprasensory world, one's clear vision of that relationship can be taken even further. This arises with an energetic suppression of the self-image one has attained. After this suppression, one's I-being may be confronted, for example, by an abyss, in which case the exercises must be continued. Or the I may find that, in its true being, it is more directly in the presence of the suprasensory world than it had been in relation to inspired knowing. In this experience, only the relationship of a suprasensory world appears to the I; in this kind of knowing, one's self is completely eliminated. If we wanted to describe this condition of mind in terms common to ordinary consciousness, we might say that one's awareness experiences itself as a stage upon which suprasensory essence—consisting of real being—not only perceives, but also is perceived.[5]

Through intuition knowledge, one's whole relationship as a human "soul" in relationship to the bodily organization is altered for the direct observation of one's inner being of soul. Before spiritual vision, the ether body appears, as it were, as a suprasensory organism differentiated within itself. One recognizes that its differentiated members are adapted in definite ways to the members of the physical bodily organization. The ether body is experienced as the essential entity, and the physical body as its "copy"—as secondary. The horizon of consciousness will seem to be determined by the lawful activity of the ether body. The coordination of phenomena within this horizon results from the activity of the differentiated members of the ether body, working toward a unity. The ether body is based on an all-embracing cosmic web of laws. Essential to the unification of its activity is a tendency to relate to something as a center, and the

---

5. In *How to Know Higher Worlds*, I called this kind of knowing "intuitive knowledge," but the ordinary meaning of *intuition* must be disregarded, since it refers to any direct, conscious feeling experience. — RUDOLF STEINER

image of this unifying tendency is the physical body. Thus the physical body proves to be an expression of the universal "I," just as the ether body expresses the macrocosmic web of laws.

This all becomes clearer when we refer to a particular fact of inner soul life. This will be done in terms of memory. Because the self has been freed from the physical organization, the spiritual researcher experiences memory in a different way than one does in ordinary consciousness. Remembering, more or less undifferentiated otherwise, is divided into parts. Initially, one becomes aware of being attracted toward an experience to be remembered, like one's attention being drawn in a particular direction. The experience is really like looking spatially toward a distant object—one that was first seen, then turned away from, and then turned toward again. Essentially, the experience pushing into memory is sensed as something that has stopped far away, within the horizon of time, and does not have to be drawn from the depths of one's soul life. This turn toward the experience pressing into memory is merely subjective at first. Once the memory actually occurs, the spiritual researcher experiences the resistance of the physical body as a reflecting surface that lifts the experience into the objective world of representations. Thus, in connection with the process of remembering, the spiritual researcher experiences an event that (subjectively perceptible) takes place within the ether body and becomes the memory when it is reflected by the physical body. The first aspect of recollection would provide only disconnected experiences of the self, but, because each memory is reflected as it is impressed upon the life of the physical body, it becomes a part of I experiences.

After all that has been said, it should be clear that the inner experience of a spiritual researcher reaches the point of seeing that the perceptible, sensory human being is a phenomenon of the suprasensory human being. One seeks awareness of that suprasensory human being—not by inference or speculation based on the given world, but by transforming one's state of mind so that it rises from sensory perception to real participation in suprasensory worlds. One thus comes to recognize a soul that is richer and fuller than ordinary consciousness.

Where this path leads with further practice cannot be more than suggested here, of course, since a thorough description would require a comprehensive treatise. For a spiritual researcher, the inner being of soul becomes the "producer," or builder, of what constitutes a single human life in the physical world. This producer shows that it has within itself—interwoven into its life as realities—the forces of many lives, not just one. What might be considered evidence of reincarnation, or repeated earthly lives, becomes a matter of real observation. What one learns about the inner core of a human life reveals, as it were, the telescoping of interrelated human personalities. And those personalities can be sensed only in the relation to those that come before and after. The one that follows always manifests as a result of another. Furthermore, in the relationship of one personality to another, there is no element of continuity; rather, there is a relationship that manifests in successive earthly lives, separated by intervening periods of purely spiritual existence. To the inner soul's observation, the periods when the core of the human being was embodied in a physical organization appear differentiated from those of suprasensory existence, because, in physical existence, the experience of the mind's content appears as though projected against the background of physical life, whereas, in the latter, it appears merged into a suprasensory element that extends into the indefinite. These remarks on so-called reincarnation were intended to present only a kind of perspective on what is opened by the preceding reflections.

Those who acknowledge the possibility that one's human self may become familiar with the core of being that is visible to suprasensory vision will also no longer consider it unreasonable to assume that, with further insight into this core of being, its content will be revealed as differentiated, and that this differentiation gives us a spiritual view of a succession of forms of existence, extending into the past. The fact that these forms of existence can carry their own time indications may be seen through the analogy of ordinary memory. An experience that appears in memory also carries its own time indication. But the real "reexamination in memory" of past forms of existence, supported by rigid self-discipline, is still very remote, of course, from the training of the spiritual researcher thus far described, and great difficulties for the inner soul life tower on the path before this can be attained with any real certainty. Nevertheless, this lies ahead on the path to knowledge just described. It has been my desire, first, to register, as it were, facts of experience of inner soul observation. Therefore, I have described reincarnation only as one such fact, but this fact can be established also on a theoretical basis. I have done this in the chapter "Destiny and the Reincarnation of the Spirit" in *Theosophy*. I tried to show that certain findings of modern natural science, if thought through to their conclusion, lead to the acceptance of human reincarnation.

Regarding the overall nature of the human being, we must conclude from this discussion that one's essential nature becomes comprehensible when viewed in terms of the interaction of the four members: first, the physical body; second, the ether body; third, the astral body; and fourth, the I. The "I" develops as this last-named body and manifests through the relationship between the central core of one's being and the physical organization. It is impossible to further articulate these four life manifestations of the whole human being within the limits of one lecture. The intention has been merely to show the basis of spiritual research. [6]

The exposition I have presented will make it clear that spiritual science, understood correctly, is based on a rigidly systematized method of developing the human soul, and that it would be wrong to imagine that the state of mind for spiritual research includes anything like what is commonly called religious fervor, ecstasy, rapture, visions, and so on. Misunderstandings sometimes arise in opposition to spiritual science exactly because of confusion between the state of mind characterized here and those other states. First, a belief is created through such confusion that there is a state of rapture in the mind of the spiritual researcher, a state of being transported beyond the presence of one's consciousness, and a kind of striving for direct instinctive visions. The truth, however, is exactly the opposite. Even more than is true of ordinary consciousness, the state of mind for spiritual researchers is far removed from what is generally called ecstatic vision and ordinary clairvoyance. Even states of mind such as those Shaftesbury mentions are vague inner worlds compared to those striven for through the practice of true spiritual research.[7] Shaftesbury finds that one can find no path to deeper knowledge by means of the "cold intellect" without the rapture of feelings. True spiritual research involves the whole mental apparatus of logic and self-aware circumspection when it seeks to transfer consciousness from the sensory to the suprasensory sphere. It cannot be accused, therefore, of disregarding the rational element of

---

6. For more on the method, see *How to Know Higher Worlds;* on the system, see *Theosophy* and *An Outline of Esoteric Science.* — RUDOLF STEINER
7. Edmund Shaftesbury (born Webster Edgerly, 1852–1926), emphatically claimed to know all the secrets of nature. His books include *Book of the Psychic Society* (1907) and *The Other Mind, Including the Science of all Phenomena and the Practice of all Forms of Human Control of Others* (1909).

knowledge. It can, however, elaborate its concepts through thinking after perception, because, in passing out of the sensory world, it always carries and retains the rational element—like a skeleton of the suprasensory experience—as an integrating aspect of all suprasensory perception.

To the modern theory of knowledge, it has increasingly become a truism that our consciousness is given only pictures (or the mere "tokens" of Helmholtz) of the transcendently real.[8] It is unnecessary to explain here how critical philosophy and physiology (the "specific sensory energies" of Johannes Müller and his adherents) have cooperated to make of such a view seem irrefutable.[9] Naive realism views phenomena within the horizon of consciousness as more than subjective representations of something objective, and, within the philosophical development of the nineteenth century, this philosophy was thought to have been discredited for good. But, the anthroposophic viewpoint would, as a matter of course, be rejected by what lies at the foundation of this view. From the critical point of view, the anthroposophic view can be considered only an impossible leap past the limits of knowledge inherent in the nature of our consciousness.

If we may reduce an immeasurable and brilliant expression of critical epistemology to a simple formula, it might be said that a critical philosopher sees pictures, or tokens, in the realities of consciousness representations, while admitting a possible relationship to a transcendental external only within the thinking

---

8. Hermann Helmholtz (1821–1894) was interested in physics, physiology, acoustic and optical perception, mathematics, and the theory of knowledge. He held the chairs of anatomy and physiology at Bonn and of physics at Berlin. His main theories were in relation to sensation and perception.
9. Johannes Peter Müller (1801—1858) German physiologist and comparative anatomist and natural philosopher who had a significant influence on the work of Helmholtz. His major work was *Handbuch der Physiologie des Menschen für Vorlesungen,* 2 vols. (1834–40).

consciousness. Such a person holds that consciousness, of course, cannot leap beyond itself, or get outside itself, so that it can plunge into a transcendental entity. Such a concept, in fact, contains something that seems self-evident, yet it rests on an assumption that we need only look into to discredit it. It seems almost paradoxical when one brings a charge of a veiled materialism against the subjective idealism just expressed. Yet, we cannot do otherwise.

Allow me to make this clear through a comparison. For example, impress a name into wax with a seal. The name, with everything pertaining to it, has been transferred by the seal into the wax. The metal of the seal itself, however, does not pass into the wax. Now, substitute the human soul life for the wax, and substitute the transcendental for the seal. It is immediately obvious that you cannot say that it is impossible for the transcendental to pass into the impression, unless you conceive of the objective essence of the transcendental as not spiritual, since this passing of a spiritual content could be conceived, analogically, with the complete transference of the name into the wax. To meet the requirement of critical idealism, you would have to assume that the transcendental essence is to be conceived in analogy with the metal of the seal. But this cannot be done, unless you make the veiled, materialistic assumption that the transcendental must pass into the impression as something material flowing across. In the event that the transcendental is spiritual, it is entirely possible that the impression could take this up. Of course, it is impossible to show here the relationship between spiritual research and the various contemporary trends in epistemology. Therefore, this effort will be made using a few rather brief observations to point out this particular concept of the theory of knowledge and its relationship to spiritual research, which must involve tremendous difficulties. It is, perhaps, not immodest to point out that a complete foundation for discrimination between philosophy and spiritual science can be obtained from two of my publications, *Truth and Knowledge* and *Intuitive Thinking As a Spiritual Path*.

Critical idealism causes a further displacement in the simple facts of consciousness because it ignores the matter of the existing relationship between cognitional content and the I. If it is assumed, a priori, that both the I and the laws of the world (reduced to the form of ideas and concepts) are outside the transcendental, it is self-evident that the I cannot leap beyond itself and must always remain outside the transcendental. But this assumption cannot be sustained in the face of an unbiased observation of the facts of consciousness. For the sake of simplicity, we will refer to the content of the cosmic web of law, insofar as this can be expressed in mathematical concepts and formulae.

The inner conformity to law in the way mathematical forms relate is acquired within consciousness, and this is then applied to empirical, factual situations. No distinction can be seen between what exists in consciousness as a mathematical concept when, on the one hand, this consciousness relates its own meaning to an empirical, concrete situation, and, on the other, when it visualizes this mathematical concept within itself in pure abstract mathematical thinking. But this signifies only that the I, with its mathematical representation, is not outside the transcendental mathematical lawfulness of phenomena, but inside. Thus, we get a better idea of the I from the perspective of the theory of knowledge—not by thinking of the I as something inside the physical body that receives impressions from outside, but by viewing the I as within the lawfulness of phenomena, and the physical body as simply a kind of mirror that reflects back to the I, through organic physical activity, the life and activity of the I outside the body in the transcendental. If, regarding mathematical thinking, one has become familiar with the thought that the I is not in the body but outside it—that one's physical activity represents only a living mirror that reflects the life of the I within the transcendental—one can find this thought epistemologically comprehensible in relation to anything that appears within the horizon of consciousness. Thus, one can no longer say that the I would have to make a leap beyond itself to enter the transcendental; rather, one would have to see that the ordinary empirical content of consciousness is related to what is truly experienced in the inner life of one's core being, just as a mirrored image is related to the real being of the person viewed in a mirror.

By thinking in this way in relation to the theory of knowledge, conflict could certainly be eliminated between natural science, with its inclination toward materialism, and spiritual research, which presupposes the spiritual. A correct way should be established for natural scientific research, in that it could investigate the laws of the physical organization, uninfluenced by interference from a spiritual way of thinking. If we want to know the laws through which a reflected image comes into existence, we must look at the laws that govern mirrors. This will determine how the viewer is reflected; it happens in various ways, depending on whether one has a flat, concave, or convex mirror. Nevertheless, the being of the one who is reflected is outside the mirror. Thus, we can see the reasons for the form of empirical consciousness in laws discovered through natural scientific research, and none of what spiritual science has to say about the inner life of our human core of being should be mixed with these laws. In natural scientific research, one correctly opposes the interference of purely spiritual viewpoints. It is natural that, in this research, there is more sympathy with explanations given in a mechanistic way than with spiritual laws. "The fact of consciousness brought about by the stimulation of brain cells does not belong in a class essentially different from that of gravity connected with matter" (Moriz Benedikt).[10] A concept such as this must be congenial to those who are comfortable with clear, natural scientific ideas

In any event, what such explanations provide through exact methodology is conceivable to natural science—it is scientifically tenable—whereas a hypotheses of directly controlled organic processes by psychic influences is scientifically indefensible. But in all of what natural science can establish, the idea mentioned (which is fundamental from the perspective of epistemology) sees only those arrangements that *reflect* the true core of the human being. This core of being, however, is not located within the physical organization, but in the transcendental. Spiritual research should thus be thought of as a way to gain knowledge of the true nature of the phenomenon reflected. Obviously, the basis of all the laws of the physical organism and those of the suprasensory would be behind this antithesis, or being and mirror.

None of this, however, is any disadvantage to one's practice of the scientific method from either direction. By maintaining this antithesis, the method would, as it were, flow into two currents that mutually illuminate and clarify each other. For it must be said that the physical organization is not a mere reflector in an absolute sense, independent of the suprasensory. After all, the reflector must be seen as the product of the suprasensory being mirrored by it. The relative reciprocal independence of the one method or the other must be supplemented by a third method that comes to meet them. It comes into the depths of the problem and can witness the synthesis of sensory and suprasensory.

10. Moriz Benedikt (1835–1920), a pioneer in the field of biomechanics and author of *Biomechanical Laws in Medicine* (San Francisco, 1903).

The confluence of two currents may be thought of as given through a further development of the mind's life, up to the intuitive cognition as described. Such a confluence is superseded only by this knowing.

It can be asserted, therefore, that an unbiased epistemology opens the way to a correct understanding of spiritual science. It leads to the theoretical conclusion that the core of the human being may exist free of the physical organization, and that it is an illusion of ordinary thinking consciousness that the I exists absolutely within the body. The I—along with the whole of one's core of being—may be seen as an entity whose experiences of the objective world are within that world itself; it receiving its experiences as reflected impressions from the physical organization. The separation of one's core of being from the physical body must, naturally, not be thought of in a spatial way; rather, it must be viewed as a relatively dynamic "state of release."

This also resolves a seeming contradiction that might arise between what we are saying here and what was previously said about the nature of sleep. In the waking state, the human core of being is fitted into the physical organization so that it is reflected through its dynamic relationship to it. In a state of sleep, however, this reflection ceases. Because ordinary awareness—in the sense presented epistemologically here—becomes possible only through the reflection, or reflected representations, it ceases during sleep. The spiritual researcher's mental state can be understood as one that has overcome the illusion of the ordinary consciousness; it begins with a life of soul through which it actually experiences the human core of being as free of the bodily organization. Everything else that is then achieved through exercises is merely a deeper entry into the transcendental, where the I of ordinary consciousness exists, although it is unaware of its own existence within the transcendental.

Spiritual research thus proves to be epistemologically conceivable. Of course, this will be acknowledged only by those who also accept the idea that the "critical theory of knowledge" is able to maintain its dogma of the impossibility of leaping over consciousness only by failing to penetrate the illusion that the human core of being is limited to the physical body and receives its impressions through the senses.

I realize that I have only outlined my exposition of epistemology. Nevertheless, it may be possible to see from these indications that they are not isolated notions, but arise from a developed, fundamental epistemological concept.

3. Suprasensory Knowledge

Those who speak of suprasensory worlds immediately open themselves to the very understandable criticism that they are violating one of the most important requirements of our time. This is the requirement that the most important questions of existence be seriously discussed only from a scientific perspective, so that science recognizes its own limitations, understanding clearly that, unless it restricts itself to the physical world of earthly existence, it would certainly degenerate into fantasy.

This is exactly the kind of spiritual scientific perception I spoke of at last year's Vienna conference of the anthroposophic movement, and will again speak of today.[1] It claims to be free of any hostility toward scientific thinking and the scientific sense of responsibility of our time, and claims to work in complete harmony with the most conscientious scientific requirements of those very people who base their work on the most rigorous natural science. Nevertheless, we can speak from various perspective about the scientific demands imposed on us today by theoretical and practical research into human evolution, which has emerged in a splendid way during the past three or four centuries, especially the nineteenth century. Therefore, I will speak today about suprasensory knowledge, insofar as it tends to fulfill exactly this demand. I want to speak in another lecture about

---

1. See Rudolf Steiner, *The Tension between East and West,* part one, "Anthroposophy and the Sciences," 5 lectures, June 1–5, 1922.

suprasensory knowledge of the human being as a requirement today of the human heart, or feelings.

Consider the magnificent contribution that scientific research has brought us, even recently—the magnificent contribution to discoveries concerning relationships throughout the external world. But it is possible to speak in a different sense about the achievements that have come about specifically in connection with this current of human evolution. For instance, we could point out that, because of conscientious and sincere natural scientific research into the principles and truths of the outer sensory world, special human capacities have been developed. And it is just such observation and experimentation that illuminates human capacities themselves. I would like to say, however, that many of those who hold positions of great respect in the field of scientific research are reluctant to notice the way their own research has shed light on humankind.

Consider what this light has illuminated; human thinking has gained immeasurably, because it has been able to investigate both close and distant relationships, the microscopic and the telescopic. It has gained discernment, comprehension, and insight to connect phenomena so that their secrets are revealed; the ability to determine the laws behind cosmic relationships; and so on. As this kind of thinking develops, we can see that standards are established for it's use and for the most serious of researchers—the requirement that thinking become as selfless as possible when observing outer nature or when experimenting in a laboratory or clinic. Human beings have achieved tremendous power in this respect. People have established more and more rules, whose nature prevents any sort of inner desires or opinions—or even fantasies about one's own being—from being carried into what one discovers about life and existence through a microscope, telescope, or various measuring devices.

Such influences have led to a kind of thinking that, one might say, has worked out its passive role with a certain inner diligence. Thinking in connection with observations and experiments has become completely abstract—so abstract that it no longer trusts the knowledge or truth of its own inner being.

It is this gradually developed quality of thinking that requires, first and foremost, a rejection of the essential, inner human being. For what we are ourselves must be presented in activity, and this can really never exist apart from the impulse of volition. Thus, we have reached the point—and this is the proper point for external research—of actually rejecting the activity of thinking, even though it is this very activity that made us aware of what it means to be human beings in the universe and within the whole of cosmic interrelationships. In a sense, human beings have eliminated themselves in their research and prohibit their own inner activity. But we will see that what is correctly prohibited in outer research must become especially developed in ourselves if we want to attain spiritual enlightenment and knowledge of the suprasensory element of our own being.

A second element in human nature, however, has been obligated to manifest a particular aspect in modern research, one that is alien to humanity, even though friendly toward the world; this is human sentiment and feeling. Human feeling is not permitted to participate in modern research; one must remain cold and matter-of-fact. Nevertheless, we might ask whether it is possible to acquire forces within this human feeling that are useful in gaining knowledge of the world. We might say, on the one hand, that inner human caprice plays a role in feelings and subjectivity, and that feeling is the source of fantasy. On the other hand, we could reply that human feeling can certainly play no distinct role as it exists mainly in everyday and scientific life. Yet, remember (as science itself must describe it to us) that, throughout evolution, the human senses have not always been what they are today. They developed from a somewhat imperfect stage to their present state, and in earlier periods they certainly did not express themselves as objectively as they do today. Thus we may have an inkling that, even in subjective feelings, there may be something that could evolve just as the human senses did, and that they might be led from an experience of our own being to a comprehension of cosmic relationships at a higher level. As we observe the withdrawal of human feeling from contemporary research, we must ask this question: Could some higher sense develop within feeling, if feeling itself were developed?

In a third aspect of the human being, we find very clearly how we are forced from a very praiseworthy scientific view to something else: this is the volitional aspect of the soul's life. Anyone who is comfortable with scientific thinking knows that it is impossible for such thinking to comprehend the relationships of the world except through the principle of cause and effect. In the most rigid way, we connect spatially adjacent phenomena; in the strictest sense, we link events that occur sequentially in time. In other words, we connect cause and effect according to inflexible rules. Those who speak as individuals who are comfortable with science—not as amateurs—know the tremendous power exerted by merely considering the realms of scientific facts in this way. They know how one is captivated by this idea of universal causality, and how one is forced to subject everything one's thinking confronts to this rule of causality.

But there is human volition—human will that says, every moment of our waking day: "What you do because of yourself— by reason of your will—is not determined causally in the sense that cause applies to external, natural phenomena." Consequently, based on immediate experience, even those who simply feel natural about themselves, and whose self-observation is unbiased, can scarcely avoid claiming a free will. But when people turn to scientific thinking, they deny free will. This is one of the conflicts people face under current conditions. We will learn more about these conflicts in these lectures. But, because we must be honest about scientific research, on the one hand, and about self-observation, on the other, this conflict completely confounds anyone who can thoroughly feel it in its full intensity, so that it might cause one to doubt the existence of any firm basis for a search for truth.

We must deal with such conflicts from the correct human perspective. We must know that research drives us to the point where we cannot admit what we are aware of every day—that there must be an approach to the world other than the one offered irrefutably by the external order of nature. Because we are driven so forcibly into such conflicts by the natural order of things, for people today it becomes necessary to admit the impossibility of talking about the suprasensory worlds as they were spoken of until quite recently. Just go back to the first half of the nineteenth century, to people who, because their consciousness was in harmony with the time, were serious in their scientific work, and yet pointed out the suprasensory aspect of human life, which opens us to a view of the divine and our own immortality. They always pointed to what we might now call the "night aspects" of human life. People who deserved the very highest regard pointed to that wonderful, though very problematic, world into which we are transported each night: the dream world. They pointed out many mysterious relationships between this chaotic imagery of dreams and the world of actuality. They have called attention to the fact that the inner nature of the human organization, especially in illness, reflects itself in fantastic dream images, and they indicated the way healthy human life enters the chaotic experiences of dreams, which take the forms of signs and symbols. They showed that much of what cannot be surveyed by people with their waking senses finds its place in a state of semi-sleep of the soul, and they drew conclusions from such matters. These things border on a subject that many still study today—that is, the subconscious human soul life, which manifests in a similar way.

But everything that appears to a person in this form might give a certain satisfaction to earlier humanity, but it is no longer valid. This is because our way of seeing outer nature has changed. Here we must recall a time when science was no more than mystical astrology. People viewed the sensory world in such a way that perception had nowhere near the precision demanded by science today. Because people did not need the completely clear senses that we have today, they were able to discover something from which they could draw inferences while in a mystical, semiconscious state. We cannot do this today. From what natural science gives us directly today, we get nothing but questions concerning true human nature. Consequently, we cannot afford to remain at the level of natural science today and expect to meet our suprasensory needs as people did in earlier times.

The form of suprasensory knowledge I am talking about involves an understanding of the needs of our times. It looks at what natural science does with human thinking, feeling, and volition and wonders if it is possible—as a result of the achievements of contemporary thinking, feeling, and the will—to further understand the suprasensory world with the same clarity that rules science. We cannot do this through inferential reasoning or logic; natural science correctly points out the limitations of such methods. Something else can happen, however: inner human capacities may evolve beyond where they stand in ordinary scientific research. Thus, in the development of our spiritual capacities, we can apply the same precision that we usually apply to laboratory and clinical research.

I will begin with thinking itself, which has become increasingly aware of its passive role in ordinary research and is unwilling to repudiate this. But thinking can energizing itself to inner activity. It can invigorate itself in such a way that, while not as precise in terms of measure and weight as in ordinary research, it is exact in terms of its own development, just as a scientist or mathematician will follow every step of research with full awareness. This can happen when the method of suprasensory cognition I have been speaking of employs exact thinking instead of an ancient, vague meditation method, or an indistinct immersion in thinking.[2]

According to one's innate capacities, individuals should discipline themselves for a period of time to trade the role of passive surrender to the outer world—which one otherwise correctly assumes in thinking—for the role of introducing one's whole inner activity of soul into clear thinking. This should be done by taking some particular thought into your mind each day, even if only for a brief period. The content of the thought is not the important matter. While withdrawing your inner nature from the outer world, direct all the powers of your soul toward inner concentration on that thought. This process leads to the development of soul capacities that we could compare to the results of developing certain muscles of the body—one's arms, for instance. One's muscles are strengthened through exercise. Likewise, one's soul capacities become more powerful by being directed toward a specific thought.

This exercise must be arranged to proceed with precision so that you watch every step in thought, just as mathematicians

---

2. Here, I can indicate only the general principles of what I have said about the exact development of thinking in my *Outline of Esoteric Science, How to Know Higher Words,* and other books. — RUDOLF STEINER

survey their processes while solving a problem in geometry or math. This can be done in a great variety of ways. It may seem trivial to say that you can select something as an object of concentration from any sort of book, even a worthless old volume that one has never seen before. The important point is not the truth of the matter, but the fact that we survey the thought completely. You cannot do this if you take a thought from memory. There are too many vague associations with such a thought in one's subconscious or unconscious, and it is impossible to be exact when concentrating on such a thought. You should fix on something entirely new in the very center of your consciousness, something that you confront only in terms of its actual content, which is not associated with any experience of the soul. The important thing is to concentrate the forces of your soul, and the increased strength that results from this.

Similarly, if you go to someone who has made progress in this area and request a thought, it is not good to entertain a prejudice against it. The content, in this case, is entirely new to you, and you can survey it. Many people are afraid that, in this way, they may come to depend on the one who provides the thought, but this is not the case. In fact, you will become less dependent than if you take such a thought out of your own memory and experience, in which case it is connected with all sorts of subconscious experiences. Furthermore, for those who have had some practice in scientific work, it is good to use the results of scientific research as material for concentration; indeed, these are the most fruitful of all for this purpose.

If you continue doing this for a relatively long time—doing it with patience and endurance, because for some it requires a few weeks or months before one succeeds, and in some cases years—you may arrive at a point where this method of shaping your thoughts can be applied with the same precision a physicist or chemist applies to measuring and weighing when researching the secrets of nature. What you learn is applied to the continued development of thinking. At a certain point, you will have an important inner experience: you will sense that you have gone beyond mere images of outer phenomena, which is true to reality in inverse proportion to the force it possesses in itself, to the degree that it is a mere picture. You reach the point of adding to this thinking an inner experience of thinking in which you live—thinking filled with inner power. This is a significant experience. Thinking becomes, as it were, something that you begin to experience, just as you experience the power of your muscles when taking hold of an object or hitting something. The kind of reality one usually experiences only in relation to breathing or muscle activity now enters your thinking. Because you have investigated every step upon the way with precision, you experience yourself with full clarity and presence of mind in strengthened, active thinking.

If one were to argue, for example, that knowledge comes only from observation and logic, this is not a real argument. After all, what you are experiencing right now is perceived with complete inner clarity, yet in such a way that your thinking also becomes a kind of "touching with the soul." In forming a thought, you "extend a feeler," but not in the way a snail extends a feeler into the physical world. Rather, it is like a feeler extended into the spirit world, which is still present only for our feelings if we have developed this far, but which we can rightly expect. You will have the feeling that your thinking has been transformed into "spiritual touch." If this feeling increases, you may expect your thinking to come into contact with a spiritual reality, just as your physical finger comes into contact with physical reality.

It is thus possible for you to progress in your exercises and reach the point where you can, as the next step, put away this soul content. You can, in a sense, empty your consciousness of what you brought into it—the thought that you concentrated upon, and that gave you real thinking involving a sense of touch for the soul. It is fairly easy in ordinary life to acquire an empty consciousness; just fall asleep. But it requires intense force to put away a specific thought after you have gotten used to concentrating on it in order to strengthen your thinking, which has now become a reality. Yet you can put aside this thought in exactly the same way you first acquired the powerful force needed for concentration. Once you have succeeded, something appears to your soul that was previously possible only as images of episodes in your memory. Your whole inner life appears in a new way before the eyes of your soul, exactly as you passed through this earthly existence since birth—or since the earliest point of time to which your memory can return, the point when you consciously entered this earthly existence.

Ordinarily, the only thing we know about this earthly existence is what we can recall from memory; we have pictures of our experiences. But the experience of strengthened thinking is not like this; it appears as a tremendous tableau. We do not recall merely a dim picture of what we passed through ten years ago, for example; we have an inner experience that, in spirit, we are retracing the course of time. If, for example, one carries out such an exercise at the age of fifty and arrives at the result indicated, time allows that individual to go back as though along a "time path," all the way to experiences at, say, the age of thirty-five. One travels back through time. It is not merely a vague memory of what one passed through fifteen years ago; one has the sense of being in the midst of it as a living reality, no different than an experience of the present moment. One travels through time, and space loses its meaning one is presented with a grand tableau of memory.

This becomes a precise picture of human life. It is the kind that appears, even according to scientific thinkers, when someone experiences great terror or severe shock (when drowning, for example), and for a few moments one's entire earthly life appears in pictures before the soul, later to be remembered with a certain shuddering fascination. In other words, what appears to the soul in such cases, as through a natural convulsion, now appears as indicated, and you are faced with your entire earthly life as a grand spiritual tableau, but in chronological order. Only now do you know yourself; only now can you truly see yourself. Once you have lived for awhile in this inwardly strengthened thinking, complete self-knowledge becomes possible. We realize then that the soul element has become, through concentration, an experiential reality.

You can differentiate this image of the inner human being from a mere picture in memory. It is clear that a memory picture is something in which people, events, or things come to us as though from outside; a memory picture is a means for the world to connect with us. The suprasensory memory tableau that appears to a person, on the other hand, confronts us as though it comes from ourselves. If, for example, you began a loving friendship with someone at a certain point of time in life, a mere memory picture shows that person arriving at a certain time, something said, what one owes to that person, and so on. But in the life tableau, you are confronted by the way you longed for that person, and how, ultimately, every step you took led inevitably to that being, whom you recognized as being in harmony with yourself.

What occurred through the development of soul forces comes to meet you with exact clarity as a life tableau. There are many who do not like such precise clarity; it enlightens them about much that they would prefer to see in a light other than the truth. But you must endure the fact that you can look at your own inner being, completely free of preconceptions, even if one's being meets the searching eye with reproach. This is the state of knowing that I call *imaginative knowledge,* or *imagination.*

One can go beyond this stage, however. The memory tableau confronts us with knowledge of the forces that formed us as human beings. You know now that forces evolve within you and form the substances of your physical body. Especially during childhood, inner forces evolved that, until about the seventh year, formed the nerves in the brain, which did not exist in a finely structured form at birth. Now you no longer believe that the formative activity in a human being arises from the forces of material substances; this ends once you face the memory tableau and see how the contents of this memory tableau flow into the forces of nutrition, breathing, and blood circulation. These are forces in themselves, without which not one wave of blood circulates, nor would a single breath occur. You gain the insight that the inner human being consists of spirit and soul.

An analogy would best describe what dawns on you. Imagine that you have walked a certain distance on rain-softened ground, and that, while walking you noticed the tracks of human feet or the wheels of a vehicle. Now imagine a being from the moon comes and sees this condition, but does not see a human being. This moon being might conclude that all sorts of underground forces created these traces and forms on the ground. Such a being might look inside the earth for the forces that seem to have produced those tracks. But anyone who can see through the matter understands that the situation was not caused by the earth but by feet or wheels.

Now, those who hold a view like the one I just described will never, because of it, look with any less reverence at, say, the brain's convolutions. Yet, just as one knows that tracks on the ground do not come from forces inside the earth, you now know that the convolutions of a brain do not come from forces inside the brain's substance, but that the spiritual psychic entity of the human being is there—which you have now seen—and that it affects the brain in such a way that it becomes convoluted. This is essential: to be shown this view, so that we reach an idea of our own spirit and soul nature, and the eye of the soul is directed toward the soul and spirit and its manifestations in outer life.

And, it is possible to progress even further. After we strengthen our inner being by concentrating on a specific thought, and after we empty our consciousness so that, instead of the images we formed, our life itself appears to us, now we can put this memory tableau out of consciousness, just as we already emptied consciousness of the individual concept. Now we can learn to apply this powerful force to rid our consciousness of what we realized through heightened self-observation as a spirit soul being. When doing this, we rid consciousness of nothing less than our own soul's inner being.

First, we learned through concentration to get rid of the outer, and then we learned to direct the soul's view to our spirit soul entity, which occupied the whole tableau of memory. Now, if we succeed in ridding ourselves of the memory tableau itself, consciousness becomes truly empty, as I wish to describe it. We have already lived in the memory tableau, or what we set up before our minds, but now something completely different arises. We have subdued what lived within us, and we now confront the world with empty consciousness. This indicates something extraordinary in the soul's experience.

Essentially, I can begin to describe what takes place only through analogy—that is, the effects of eliminating the content of our soul when we apply a powerful inner force. Just consider the fact that, once the impressions of the external senses have died away, when seeing or hearing ceases, or perhaps even one's distinct sense of touch, we sink into a state closely resembling sleep. But now, when we eliminate the soul's content, we come to an empty state of consciousness, though not a state of sleep. We reach what I might call a state of "simple wakefulness"— awake, but with an empty consciousness.

We might think of this empty consciousness as follows: imagine a noisy, modern city. As we withdraw from the city, everything around us becomes more and more quiet. Finally, we arrive, say, deep in a forest, where we find the absolute opposite of the city's noises and live in the complete inner stillness of hushed peace. Now, to describe what follows, I must resort to a trivial analogy. We must ask whether this peace and stillness can be changed even further into something else. We will call the stillness the "zero point" in our perception of the external world. If we own a certain amount of property and then subtract from it, the property is diminished; if we take away more, it is further diminished, and eventually we arrive at zero, with nothing remaining. Can we now go even farther? It may be undesirable to most people, but in fact many do this: they decrease what they own by incurring debt. One then has less than zero and can still diminish what one has. In exactly the same way, we can at least imagine that the stillness—like the zero point of being awake—can be pushed beyond zero to a kind of negative state. A "super-stillness," a super-peace may augment the quiet. This is the experience of having blotted out your own soul content: in your soul, you enter a state of quietness below the zero point. It is the most intense inner stillness of soul that comes about during this state of wakefulness.

This cannot be attained, however, without something else. It arises only when you sense that a certain state, linked with the images of your own self, is transformed into another state. One who senses and contemplates the first level of one's suprasensory inner self experiences a certain sense of well-being and inner blissfulness. This is what the various religions refer to by pointing to the suprasensory realm and reminding us that it brings us an experience of inner bliss. Indeed, until one has eliminated one's own inner self, there is a sense of well-being, an intense feeling of bliss. At that moment, however, when a stillness of soul arises, inner well-being is completely replaced by inner pain, or deprivation, such as you have never known; it is the sense that you have been separated from everything you were connected to in earthly life—far removed not only from feeling your own body, but from feeling your own experiences since birth. And this means a deprivation that increases to a frightful pain of soul. Many people shrink from this stage; they cannot find the courage to cross from a lower clairvoyance, after eliminating their soul content, to a state of inner stillness. If you enter this stage in full awareness, however, *imagination* is replaced by what I have called *inspiration* in the books already mentioned (I trust you will not be offended by these terms). It is the experience of a real spiritual world. Once you have eliminated the sensory world and established an empty consciousness, which is accompanied by inexpressible pain of soul, the outer spirit world comes to meet you. In the state of *inspiration,* you become aware that human beings are surrounded by a spirit world, just as the sensory world exists for the outer senses.

The first thing that you see in this spirit world is your own existence before birth. Just as you are usually aware of earthly experiences through ordinary memory, now cosmic memory dawns; you look into your experiences before birth and see what you were like as a spirit and soul being in a purely spiritual world before descending to be born into this earthly existence—when, as spirit beings, you participated in the formation of your body.

This is how you look back at the spirit, or eternal, in human nature. It is revealed to you as your existence before birth, which you now know does not depend on physical birth and death, because it existed before birth and before conception and formed a human being out of a physical body taken from matter and heredity.

For the first time you also reach a true idea of physical heredity, because you can see the suprasensory forces that play into it—forces you acquired from a purely spiritual world that you now feel united with, just as you feel united with the physical world in ordinary earthly life. Furthermore, you become aware of the fact that, despite the great advances in human evolution, much has been lost that was inherent to the ancient, instinctive concepts that we are no longer able to use today. The instinctive suprasensory sight of earlier humanity was confronted by this pre-earthly life, as well as by human immortality (about which we will speak later). In ancient times, eternity was thought of in such a way that one understood both of its aspects. Today, we talk of the immortality of a human soul—in fact, our language possesses only this word. But people once spoke of the "unborn" (and the more ancient languages continue to show such words), which is the other aspect of the human soul's eternity. Today, however, the times have changed somewhat. People are interested in the question of what happens to the human soul after death, because it is still to come; but the question of what existed before birth or conception is less interesting, because that is in the past, and yet we are here. True knowledge of human immortality, however, arises only when we consider eternity in both of its aspects: immortality and the unborn.

But, to maintain a connection with the unborn—especially in an exact clairvoyance—something else is needed. We sense ourselves as truly human when we no longer permit our feelings to be absorbed completely into earthly life. What we begin to understand as our life before birth now penetrates us as pictures, and this is added to what we previously felt as our humanity. It makes us, for the first time, completely human. Our feelings are shot through with inner light, and we now realize that we have developed our feelings into a sensory organ for the spirit.

But you must go even further and be able to make your volition into an organ of knowledge for the spirit. To do this, something must begin to play a role in human knowledge that, very correctly, is otherwise not considered to be a way of knowledge by those who wish to be taken seriously in the field of cognition. You first become aware that this is a way of knowledge when you enter the suprasensory realms. It is the force of *love.* However, you must begin to develop this force of love in a higher sense than that given to us by nature, although that form is important for nature and human life.

My description of the first steps toward developing a higher form of love in human life may seem paradoxical. When you try to see the world with new awareness—with real circumspection for each step—you reach a higher love. Suppose that, in the evening before sleep, you endeavor to bring your day's life into your awareness. You begin with the last event of the evening, visualizing it as precisely as possible, then likewise visualize the next previous event, then the next, thus moving backward to morning in your survey of the day's events. In this process, the inner energy expended is more important than whether you visualize each occurrence with relative precision. The important thing is the reversed order of visualization. Ordinarily, we consider the earlier events first, and then the later ones in a consecutive chain. Through this exercise, you reverse your whole life; you think and feel in a direction that is opposite to the course of your day. You can practice this on the experiences of your day, as suggested, which requires only a few minutes, but you can also do this in a different way. Visualize the course of a drama, so that you begin with the fifth act, imagining it advancing forward through the fourth and third, all the way to the beginning. Or you can think of a melody in the reversed order of notes.

As you go through more and more inner soul experiences like this, you discover that your inner experience is freed from the outer course of nature, and that you become increasingly self-directed. But, although you will become more and more individualized and achieve an increasing power of self-direction, you also learn to pay attention to your outer life with greater awareness. Now do you become aware that, as you develop more powerfully through practicing this conscious absorption in another being, you must compensate with a higher degree of selflessness and greater love. Thus, you feel how this experience of not living in yourself but in another being—passing from your own being to another—becomes more and more powerful. You reach a stage where, to *imagination* and *inspiration,* which you have already developed, you can now add a truly intuitive ascension into another being: you reach *intuition,* no longer experiencing only yourself, but also learn—as a complete individual, yet with complete selflessness—to experience the other being.

Love gradually makes it possible for you to look back even farther than your pre-earthly spirit life. As you learn in your present life to look back at contemporary events, by elevating love you learn to look back at former earthly lives and to recognize the whole life of a human being as not one, but a succession of earthly lives.[3] We come to know the human life, however, as a

---

3. The fact that those various earthly lives had a beginning and, likewise, a necessary end will be discussed another time. — RUDOLF STEINER

succession of lives on earth, between which there are always intervening spiritual lives, between death and the next birth.

This elevated love, lifted to the spirit realm and transformed into a force of knowledge, also teaches us the true meaning of death. Once you have advanced (as explained in terms of *imagination* and *inspiration*) to the point of making these intensified inner forces capable of spiritual love, you will truly come to know, through direct, precise clairvoyance, the inner experience of experiencing yourself spiritually, outside the body. Leaving the body in this way becomes, as it were, an objective soul experience. Once you have clairvoyantly experienced this spiritual existence outside of the body, you will know the significance of laying aside the physical body at death and passing through the portal of death to a new, spiritual life. We learn, at the third stage of exact clairvoyance, the significance of death, and thus also the significance of human immortality.

I know very well that, regardless of the motive, anyone who presents something to the world as a "requirement of the time" also implies a certain self-importance. This is not my purpose; rather, I would like to demonstrate that the demands of our time already exist, and that the very step taken by spiritual science is an attempt to meet those demands. We may say, then, that spiritual scientists, whom we wish to discuss, do not wish to present themselves as people with superficial views. Rather, they try to advance in real harmony with natural science and with the same genuine awareness. They desire exact clairvoyance to describe the spiritual world.

They also know, however, that, whenever one investigates a human corpse in a laboratory to explain its former life, or if one looks out to cosmic space with a telescope, one develops capacities that were initially adapted only to the microscope or telescope, but they have an inner life and misrepresent their expression. If we dissect a human body, we know that it was not nature that directly created this human being in this form, but that it was made by the human soul, which has already withdrawn. We interpret the human soul from its physical product, and it would be irrational to assume that the formation of human physical forces and substance did not arise from what preceded the present state of this human being. As we investigate dead nature, however, with forces from which one properly withdraws one's inner activity, from that very act of holding back, an ability is created to further develop human soul forces.

Just as the seed of a plant lies hidden beneath the earth after it is planted and will nevertheless become a plant, similarly, we plant a seed in the soul through the very action of conscientious scientific research. Those who are serious scientists in this sense hold the seed of *imaginative, inspired,* and *intuitive* knowledge; they only need to develop that seed. They will know that, just as natural science is a requirement of our time, suprasensory research is also necessary. In other words, anyone who speaks in the spirit of natural science also speaks in the spirit of suprasensory research, but without realizing it. There is an unconscious longing in the innermost depths of many today for this seed of suprasensory research to develop (as will be shown in another public lecture).

I have attempted to make it very clear through my method of explanation that, when we introduce the means of suprasensory cognition I am speaking of, it supplements human cognitional capacities with something that works effectively, step by step. A natural scientist applies this precision to external experimentation and observation, hoping to see things juxtaposed so that they reveal their secrets with exactness in the process of quantification. Spiritual scientists, of whom I am speaking, apply this precision to the development of their own soul forces. To use an expression of Goethe, their inner discovery, through which the spirit world and human immortality step before one's soul, is made in a precise way. With every step of a spiritual scientist toward revealing the spiritual world to the eyes of the soul, one feels obligated to perceive conscientiously, just as a mathematician must at every step. And just as mathematicians must see clearly into everything they write down, spiritual scientists likewise look with absolute precision at everything they uncover through powers of cognition. They understand that they have developed the soul's eye from the soul itself, using the same inner laws that nature uses to form physical eyes from bodily substance. They know they can speak of spirit worlds with the same authority one uses when speaking of the sensory world seen with physical eyes. In this sense, the spiritual research we are discussing satisfies the requirements of the magnificent achievements of natural science—which spiritual science in no way opposes, but seeks to supplement.

To those, therefore, who oppose spiritual research from a so-called scientific perspective, one would like to say, without ill will, that this recalls a line in Goethe's *Faust,* well known, but applied here in a different sense:

> Most folks never sense the Devil,
> Though he holds them by the collar.[4]

I don't want to go into it now, but this saying confronts us with a certain twist in the demand of our time: those who speak correctly about nature today are really expressing the spirit, though unconsciously. We can say that there are many who do not wish to notice the "spirit" when it speaks, although they are constantly expressing spirit in their own words.

---

4. Mephistopheles: "Den Teufel spürt das Völkchen nie, / Und wenn er sie beim Kragen hätte." (*Faust,* part 1).

The seed of suprasensory perception is, in fact, far more wide-spread today than imagined, but it must be developed. The fact that it must be developed is really a lesson we can learn from the serious nature of the time in terms of external experiences. As I said, I would like to go into detail another time, but we may nevertheless add in conclusion that the elements of a frightening catastrophe really speak to all of humanity today through various indications in the outer world, and that it is possible to realize the tasks that humanity will have to work at in the immediate future, which will struggle to birth with great intensity from this seriousness of the time. This serious situation in the world that confronts us today, especially the world of humanity, demonstrates the need for an inner seriousness.

Today, I wanted to speak of this inner seriousness in the guidance of human hearts and minds toward our own spiritual forces, which make up the powers of our essential being. If it is true that we must apply our most powerful outer forces in meeting the serious events that await us throughout the world, we will likewise need strong inner courage. Such forces and courage, however, will manifest only when people are able to develop the feeling and the will to self-knowledge—with complete inner awareness—not just theoretically but in practice. This is possible only when we recognize that our being emerges from its true source, the spirit—when, not just theoretically, we come to know through experience that the human being is spirit. Thus, people can find true satisfaction only in the spirit; our highest powers and greatest courage come to us only from the spirit, the suprasensory.

4. The Attainment of
Spiritual Knowledge

In response to the kind invitation to speak this evening, I would like to tell you how it is possible, through direct investigation, to acquire the spiritual knowledge we propose to study here and apply to education. Today, I will deal with the methods whereby suprasensory worlds may be investigated, and another time it may be possible to discuss some results of suprasensory research. Apart from this, however, let me add that everything I want to say refers to investigating spirit worlds, not how we understand the facts revealed by suprasensory knowledge. Such facts have been investigated and communicated, and they can be understood by any healthy, intelligent person, as long as one is unbiased enough not to base one's conclusions solely on so-called proof, logic, and so on, in regard to the outer sensory world. Because of such hindrances, it is often said that, unless we can investigate suprasensory worlds, we cannot understand the results of suprasensory research.

We are dealing with what may be called *initiation knowledge,* which was cultivated during ancient periods of human evolution in a somewhat different form than what should be encouraged today. Our aim, as I have said elsewhere, is to follow a path of research that leads to suprasensory worlds through thinking and perception that is proper to our own age—not to revive something old. In the case of initiation knowledge, everything depends on being able to fundamentally reorient the whole life of the human soul. Those who have acquired initiation knowledge are different from those with knowledge in the modern sense of the word, and not just because initiation knowledge is a higher level of ordinary knowledge. It is gained, of course, on the basis of ordinary knowledge, which must be present as a foundation. Intellectual thinking must be developed fully if one wishes to attain initiation knowledge. Then, however, a fundamental reorientation is needed, because those who possesses initiation knowledge necessarily see the world from an entirely different perspective.

In a simple formula, I can express how initiation knowledge differs fundamentally from ordinary knowledge. As the subjects of ordinary cognition, we are aware of thinking and the inner experiences whereby we acquire knowledge. We think, for example, and believe we understand something through our thoughts. When we think of ourselves as thinking beings, we are the subject. We look for objects when we observe nature and human life, and we experiment in this way; we always look for objects, and those objects must make an impression on us. Objects must surrender to us, so that we can understand them through our thinking, which we apply to them. We are the subject; what comes to us is the object.

An entirely different orientation arises in those who reach for initiation knowledge. They have to realize that, as human beings, they are the object, and that they must look for the subject in relation to the human object. Consequently, the complete reverse must begin. In ordinary knowledge, we sense that we are the subject and look for the objects outside. In initiation knowledge, we are the object, and we look for the subject—or, more accurately, in true initiation knowledge the subject appears on its own. But that is a matter of a later stage of knowledge.

So you see, even this rather theoretical definition shows that, in terms of initiation knowledge, we must, in fact, take flight from ourselves—become like plants, stones, or lightning and thunder, which are objects to us. In initiation knowledge, we slip out of ourselves, as it were, and become an object that looks for its subject. To use a somewhat paradoxical expression—in this particular reference to thinking—in ordinary knowledge, we think about things; in initiation knowledge we must discover how our being is "thought" in the cosmos. These are merely abstract principles, but you will find them pursued everywhere in the concrete data of the initiation method.

For now we are dealing only with the form of initiation knowledge that is proper for our age, and it begins with thinking. Today, thought must be fully developed if you wish to attain initiation knowledge, and a good training for this is to deeply study the growth and development of natural science in recent centuries, especially during the nineteenth century. People approach the quest for scientific knowledge in various ways. Some absorb what science has to teach with a kind of naïveté, hearing how organic beings supposedly evolved from the simplest, most primitive forms up to humankind. These individuals form ideas about evolution, but pay little attention to their own being and the fact that they have their own ideas and, in their very perception of outer processes, are developing a life of thinking.

There are some, however, who cannot accept the whole body of scientific knowledge without looking critically at themselves. They reach the point of asking what it is they are doing as they follow the development of beings from an imperfect to a perfected level. Or, people may realize that, when they work on mathematics, their thoughts evolve purely out of themselves. Mathematics, in a very real sense, is a web that you spin from your own being. When you bring this web to bear on things in the outer world, it fits. Here we come to what I must say is the great and tragic question that faces any thinker: What is thinking itself, which I apply to every kind of knowledge? Our contemplation does not allow us to discover the nature of thought, because thinking simply remains at the same level. We merely revolve around the axle we already formed. We must do something else with thinking, using methods I described as meditation in my book *How to Know Higher Worlds*.

You should not have any mystical ideas about meditation, nor should you think it is easy. Meditation must be completely clear, in the modern sense. Patience and inner soul energy are needed, and, above all, it depends on an act that no one else can do for you: it requires an inner resolve that you stick to. When you begin to meditate, you are performing the only completely free activity there is in human life. We always have within us a tendency toward freedom, and, furthermore, we have attained a large measure of freedom. But if you think about it, you find that you depend on heredity for one thing, on education for another, and on life itself. Ask yourself where we would be if we suddenly abandoned everything given to us by heredity, education, and life in general. If we suddenly abandoned all this, we would face a void. But suppose you begin to meditate regularly, in the morning and evening, so that you learn gradually to look into the suprasensory world. It is something we can choose not to do on any given day; nothing would prevent it. And, in fact, experience shows that most of those who enter a life of meditation with wonderful resolutions abandon it very soon. We have complete freedom in this, because meditation is, by its very nature, a free act. But, if you remain true to yourself and make an inner promise—not to someone else, but to yourself—to remain steadfast in your resolve to meditate, then this in itself becomes a powerful force in your soul.

Having said this, I want to speak of meditation in its simplest forms, since here I must deal only with principles. You must place at the center of your consciousness a certain idea or combination of ideas. The content is unimportant, but it must not represent something from memory. This is why, instead of taking a meditation from your own memory, it is good to let another— someone experienced in such things—give you a meditation. Not because the other has any desire to exercise any power of suggestion, but because in this way you can be sure that the substance of the meditation is entirely new to you. It is an equally good idea to take some ancient work that you have never read, and look in it for some passage to meditate upon. The point is not to draw the passage from the realm of your unconscious or subconscious, which is likely to influence you. You cannot be certain about anything from that realm, because it will be colored by the remains of past perceptions and feelings. The substance of a meditation must be as clear and pure as a mathematical formula.

Consider this sentence as a simple example: "Wisdom lives in the light." At the beginning, you cannot test the truth of this. It is an image. But you are not concerned with the intellectual meaning of the words, but must contemplate them inwardly, in the soul; you must rest in them with your consciousness. At first, you will be able to rest in this content for only a short period of time, but the period of time will become longer and longer.

The next stage involves bringing your whole soul life together to concentrate all your forces of thinking and perception on the subject of the meditation. Just as the muscles of one's arm grow strong by using them for work, soul forces are strengthened when they are repeatedly directed toward the same subject of meditation for months or even years. Your soul forces must be strengthened and invigorated before you can truly investigate the suprasensory world.

If you continue to practice in this way, a day comes—a great day—when you make a certain observation. You will perceive a soul activity that is completely independent of the body. You realize that you are now involved in an activity of soul and spirit that is absolutely free from any bodily influence, whereas before, your thinking and sentient life depended on the body—thinking depended on the nervous system, feelings on the circulatory system, and so on. You gradually notice that, in your head, something is creating a kind of vibration, which had previously been totally unconscious. You now discover, remarkably, the real difference between the sleeping and waking—the fact that when you are awake, there is a vibration throughout the whole human organism, with the exception of the head. What moves in other parts of the body is at rest in the head.

You will understand this better if I point to the fact that human beings are not, as we generally think, made up only of a robust, solid body. We are, in fact, made up of approximately ninety per cent fluid, and the amount of solid constituents immersed and swimming in those fluids is only about ten per cent. Nothing definite can be said about the amount of solid constituents in a human being. We are composed of about ninety per cent so-called water, and air and warmth pulses through a certain portion of this fluid.

If you picture the human being as having less solid body and a greater amount of water, air, and the vibrating warmth, you will not find it so unlikely that there is something even finer within us—something I will call the "ether body." This ether body is finer than the air—indeed, so fine and ethereal that it permeates our being without our awareness of it in ordinary life. It is this ether body that, in our waking life, is filled with inner, regulated movement throughout the human organism, with the exception of the head. Within the head, the ether body is at rest.

In sleep it is different. Sleep begins and then continues in such a way that the ether body begins to move also in the head. In sleep, our whole being, including the head, is permeated by an inwardly moving ether body. When we dream, perhaps just before waking, we become aware of the last movements in the ether body, which present themselves as dreams. When we awake naturally, we remain aware of those final movements of the ether body in the head. But, of course, when one is suddenly awakened, this cannot happen.

Those who persist in the method of meditation I have indicated will gradually be able to form images in the tranquil ether body of the head. In *How to Know Higher Worlds,* I call these pictures *imaginations.* They are experienced in the ether body, independently of the physical body, are the first suprasensory impressions that we can experience. They allow you, completely apart from the physical body, to perceive images of the activities and flow of your life, back to birth. There is a phenomenon often described by those who have almost drowned: they see their life backward as a series of moving images. This can be deliberately and systematically cultivated as a capacity, so that you witness all the events of your present earthly life.

The first thing that initiation knowledge provides is a view of your soul life, and it proves to be completely different from what one generally imagines. One usually thinks, in the abstract, that one's soul life is a weaving of ideas. But when you discover its true nature, you find that it is creative—that it was at work during your childhood, forming and shaping the brain, and that it now permeates your whole organism and produces a malleable, formative activity that, each day, enlivens your waking consciousness, and even your digestive processes.

We see this active inner principle in the human organism as the ether body. It is not a spatial body, but a "time body." Thus, you cannot describe the ether body in terms of a spatial form, which would be like painting a flash of lightning. When you paint lightning, you are freezing an instant. This also applies to the human ether body. In truth, we have a physical, spatial body and a temporal body, the ether body, which is always in movement. We cannot speak intelligently about the ether body unless we experience it as a time body that appears to us in an instant, and at the same time as a continuous tableau of events reaching back to birth. This is something we can discover as a suprasensory capacity in ourselves.

The effect of these inner processes on the soul's evolution (which I have described) manifests primarily as a total change of soul disposition in those who reach for initiation knowledge. Please understand what I am saying. I don't mean that those who approach initiation are suddenly transformed completely. On the contrary, modern initiation knowledge must leave us wholly in the world and able to continue life, just as we did when we began. But in the hours and moments dedicated to suprasensory investigation, initiation knowledge makes you completely different from what you are in ordinary life.

Above all, I would like to emphasize an important moment that distinguishes initiation knowledge. The more you press forward in your experience of the suprasensory world, the more you sense that the influences of your own physicality are diminishing in relation to matters involving the physical body in ordinary life. Consider how our judgments occur in life. As children, we develop and grow. Sympathy and antipathy become firmly rooted in life—likes and dislikes toward natural phenomena and, even more so, toward other people. Your body participates in all this. Sympathy and antipathy are, to a large extent, based in your physical processes and become involved very naturally into all these matters. As you approach initiation, the moment you rise to the suprasensory world, you enter a realm in which the sympathy and antipathy related to the physical body become increasingly foreign to you. You are removed from all that your corporeality connects you with. And when you wish to take up ordinary life again, you must, as it were, deliberately reinvest yourself in your ordinary sympathies and antipathies, which would otherwise occur naturally. When you awake in the morning, you live in your body and develop the same love for things and others, the same sympathies or antipathies you had the day before. If you have been for awhile in the suprasensory world and wish to return to your sympathies and antipathies, you must struggle to do so and, as it were, immerse yourself into your physicality. This removal from your physical nature is one of the signs that you have progressed. Big-hearted sympathies and antipathies begin to develop gradually in those who take the path to initiation.

In a sense, spiritual development reveals itself very strongly— in the activity and power of remembering during initiation knowledge. In ordinary life, we experience ourselves; our memory is sometimes a little better, sometimes a little worse, but we win our memories through our experiences, which we remember later. This is not true of your experiences in the suprasensory worlds. You can experience greatness, beauty, and meaning, but it is experienced, then it is gone. It must be experienced again before it can stand again before your soul. Suprasensory experience does not impress itself in the memory in the ordinary sense. It impresses itself only when you can, with tremendous effort, first conceptualize what you see in the suprasensory world, and thus transfer your understanding to the suprasensory world. This is very difficult. You must be able to think while there, but without the help of your physical body. Consequently, your concepts must be well-grounded ahead of time; you must have developed a logical, orderly mind that does not forget logic when looking into the suprasensory world. People who possess primitive clairvoyant faculties can see much, but they forget logic while there. And so, when you have to communicate suprasensory facts to others, this is especially the time you must be aware of this change in the memory in relation to spiritual truths. It shows us how much our physical body is involved in memory—memory, not thinking, which is, in fact, always involved in the suprasensory.

If I am allowed to say something personal, when I give a lecture, it is different from the way others give lectures. Usually, what people say is taken from memory; what one learns, what one thinks, is usually developed from the memory. But those who are truly unfolding suprasensory truths must "bring them to birth" in that very instant. I can give the same lecture thirty, forty, or fifty times, and for me it is never the same. Of course this may happen in other cases, too, but the power to be free of ordinary memory is greatly enhanced once this stage of inner development is attained.

You must always be able to return, however. This is essential, otherwise you become an inactive, vague mystic and a dreamer, not one who knows suprasensory worlds. You must be able to live in the higher worlds, but at the same time be able to bring yourself back and stand firmly on your own two feet. This is why, in speaking of these things, I state emphatically that for me, just as for a good philosopher, knowing, for example, how shoes and coats are sewn is almost more important than logic is. A true philosopher should be practical. You must not spend time thinking about life if you cannot live as a practical human being. And in the case of those who seek suprasensory knowledge, this is even more important. Knowers of the suprasensory cannot be dreamers or fanatics who do not stand firmly on their own two feet. Otherwise, you can lose yourself, because one must actually come out of the self, and such externalizing must not lead to becoming lost.

An Outline of Esoteric Science was written from this knowledge. What I have said concerns the ability to bring form to the ether body in the head, which makes it possible to see the time, or ether, body back to your birth, bringing about a certain frame of mind in relation to the cosmos. You lose your own corporeality, so to speak, but you gradually become accustomed to the cosmos. Your consciousness expands into the wide spaces of the ether. You no longer contemplate a plant without entering its processes of growth. You follow it from root to blossom and live in its fluids, flowering, and fruiting. You can steep yourself in the life of animals as revealed by their forms, but primarily in the life of other human beings. The slightest trait perceived in others will lead you into their whole soul life, so that during such suprasensory perception you feel not inside, but outside yourself.

The question then becomes one of whether you can take this suprasensory knowledge even further. This occurs through cultivating your meditation. To begin with, you rest in meditation on certain specific ideas, or a combination of ideas, and thus strengthen your life of soul. But this is not sufficient to enter the suprasensory world fully; another exercise is needed. Not only is it necessary to rest with specific ideas, concentrating your whole soul on them, but you must also be able to will those ideas out of your consciousness. In physical life, you can look at an object and then away from it; similarly, in esoteric development you must learn to concentrate on some idea and then to drive it away completely.

Even in ordinary life this is difficult. Just think how little most people have under their control—always compelled by thoughts. Thoughts often haunt a person day in and day out, especially when they are unpleasant. One cannot get rid of them. This is even more difficult to do when you have gotten accustomed to concentrating on a particular thought. The object of your concentration finally begins to take hold, and you must exert great effort to drive it away. After long practice, however, you will be able to throw it entirely from your consciousness—the whole retrospective tableau of life back to birth, the whole ether body I have called the time body.

This is, of course, a stage of development you must advance toward. First, you must mature. By sweeping away the ideas on which you have meditated, you gain the power to rid yourself of that colossus in the soul—the terrible specter of life, from the present moment back to birth, which stands there and must be done away with. Once you eliminate it, a more wakeful awareness arises in you. Consciousness fully awakens, but it is empty. Then it begins to fill. Just as air streams into your lungs when they need it, the true spiritual world flows into this empty consciousness, just as I have described it.

This is *inspiration*. It is an influx, but not of some finer substance; it is something related to substance, just as negative is to positive. The reverse of substance begins to pour into your human nature, which has become free of the ether. It is important to become aware that spirit is not just a finer, more ethereal substance. If we speak of substance as positive, we speak of spirit as being the negative to the positive.[1] Let me put it this way: imagine that I have five dollars. If I give one dollar away, I then

---

1. We could also speak of substance as negative, but that is not the point; such matters are relative. — RUDOLF STEINER

have four dollars left. If I give another away, I have only three dollars, and so on until I have no more. But then I borrow, and if I owe someone a dollar, I have less than none. If I have eliminated the ether body through the methods described, I do not find a finer ether, but the reverse of ether, just as debts are the reverse of assets.

Now I know spirit through experience. Spirit pours into you through *inspiration*; the first thing you experience now is your soul and spirit in a spiritual world before birth and before conception. This is the pre-earthly life of your soul and spirit. Before reaching this point, you saw into the ether, all the way back to birth. Now you look beyond conception and birth, into the world of soul and spirit, and you see yourself as you were before coming from spiritual worlds and acquiring a physical body from a line of heredity. In *initiation* knowledge these are not philosophical truths that you merely think through—they are experiences that must be earned by using the preparations discussed. The first truth that arises when you enter the spiritual world is that of the pre-earthly existence of the human soul and the human spirit respectively. You now learn to see the eternal directly.

For many centuries, Europeans have been able to conceive of only one aspect of eternity, that of immortality. People have asked only about what happens to the soul after it leaves the body at death. This question is an egoistic privilege, because the interest in what comes after death arises from an egoistic perspective. You will see that we can speak of immortality, too, but most discussion of it is based on egoism. People are less interested in what preceded birth; they say, "We are here now. What proceeded this is merely something to know." But you cannot gain the real value of such knowledge unless you try to view existence as it was before conception.

We need a modern word that completes the idea of eternity. We should not speak only of immortality without also speaking of *the unborn,* a term that is difficult to translate. Eternity has these two aspects: immortality and the unborn. And initiation knowledge discovers the unborn before immortality.

Another level along the path to the suprasensory world can be reached if you now try to make your activity of soul and spirit freer of the body's support. To this end, you gradually guide the meditation and concentration exercises to become volitional exercises. As a concrete example, let me describe a simple exercise for strengthening the will. It will help you to study the principle involved. In ordinary life, we are accustomed to thinking along with the course of the world. We allow things to come as they occur. We think first of what comes earlier, and think later about what comes later. And even if we do not think with the course of time in more logical thought, there is always a background tendency to stick with the outer, more concrete course of events. Now, to exercise our forces of spirit and soul, we must get free of that outer course of phenomena. A good exercise (one that is also an exercise for the will) is to try to think back through your day's experiences—not as they occurred from morning to evening, but backward, from evening to morning, going into as much detail as you can.

Suppose in this reversed review that you come to a moment when, during the day, you climbed some stairs. You will think of yourself at the top, then at the step before the top, and so on to the bottom. You go down that staircase backward in thought. To begin with, you will be able to visualize only short episodes of the day in this backward order, say from six o'clock back to three, or from twelve to nine, and so on to the moment of awaking. Gradually, however, you will acquire a kind of technique, so that, in the evening or the next morning, you will be able to let a retrospective tableau of the day's experiences or those of the day before pass before your soul in pictures. If you can completely free yourself (and you will come to this) from thinking that follows three-dimensional reality, you will see a tremendous power grow in the will. You will also reach this point if you can acquire the ability to experience the notes of a melody backward, or visualize a drama in five acts, beginning with the fifth, then the fourth, and so on to the first act. Through such exercises, the will is strengthened, because you inwardly invigorate it and loosen it from bondage to events in the material world.

Again, these exercises can be appropriate if you take stock of yourself and recognize this or that habit that you have acquired. You must take hold of yourself and apply an iron will to change, in a couple of years or so, a certain habit into a different one. For example, a suggestion of character may be seen in a person's handwriting. It takes great effort and a strong inner force to change your handwriting so that it bears no resemblance to what it was before. That second form of handwriting must become just as much a habit and as fluid as the first. This is a trivial example, and there are many matters whereby the fundamental direction of will may be changed with effort. Gradually, you reach the point where not only is the spiritual world received in us as *inspiration*, but your spirit, freed from the body, is submerged in other spiritual beings outside of you. True spiritual knowledge means submerging yourself in spirit beings, who are all around us any time we look back at physical phenomena. To know the spiritual, you must first, as it were, get outside of yourself. I have already described this. You must also gain the ability to "sink" into things—that is, into spiritual beings.

We can do this only after we have practiced the kinds of initiation exercises I have described. They will bring us to the point where our body no longer disturbs us, and instead we are able to submerge ourselves in the spiritual nature of phenomena, so that the colors of plants no longer merely appear to us, but we plunge into those colors; we do not merely color plants, but watch them color themselves. When we contemplate a chicory blossom along the road, we not only see that it is blue, but, inwardly, we can submerge ourselves in the blossom and in the process that makes it blue. From this point, we can continually extend spiritual knowledge.

There are various indications that show whether these exercises have been a means of real progress. I will mention two, but there are many. One indication is that we gain a way of seeing morality in a completely new way. To the intellect alone, there is something unreal about the world of morality. Of course, if a person must obey the laws of decent behavior in an age of materialism, it will be felt necessary to do what is right according to traditions. But even though it's not acknowledged, one thinks, "I do what is right; it doesn't have the same reality as, say, lightning or thunder rolling across the sky." It does not seem real in the same sense. But when you live in the spiritual world, you become aware that the moral world order not only has all the reality of the physical world, but a higher reality. Gradually, you come to understand that this entire era, along with all its phenomena, could disintegrate, but that the moral influences that flow out of us maintain their power. The reality of the moral world dawns upon us. The physical and the moral worlds— being and becoming—become one. We have a concrete experience that the world has both moral laws and objective laws.

This increases responsibility toward the world. It gives you a completely different awareness, one that people sorely need today. Modern humankind looks back to the earth's beginning, when the earth was supposedly formed from a primal mist. Life is believed to have arisen from that same mist, then humanity, and, like a mirage, the world of ideas from the human being. Human-kind looks forward to a death of warmth—a time when all that humankind lives within must be submerged in a great tomb—and people must come to know the moral world order, which, fundamentally, can be comprehended only by gaining true spiri-tual knowledge, which I can give you only in a brief outline.

Another indication of progress is that one cannot reach *intui-tive* knowledge—the ability to submerge oneself in outer things—without passing through suffering much more intense than the pain I spoke of in relation to *imagination*, when I said that, through your own effort, you must find the way back into your sympathies and antipathies. This inevitably means pain. But now, pain becomes a cosmic experiencing of all the suffering that rests on the ground of being.

One can easily ask why the gods, or God, created suffering in the first place. But, suffering must exist before the world can arise in all its beauty. The fact that we have eyes is simply because, in a primitive, still undifferentiated organism, organic forces were excavated that lead to sight, and that, in their final transforma-tion, become the eye. If today we were still aware of the minute processes that take place in the retina as sight, we would realize that even this event is essentially a latent pain. All beauty is grounded in suffering. Beauty can be developed only from pain. And one must be able to experience the pain and suffering. Only by going through this pain do we truly find our way into the suprasensory world. This can already be said, to a lesser extent, of a lower level of knowledge. Those who have gained even a little knowledge will admit that, I have my destiny to thank for the good fortune and happiness I have in life; but I have been able to acquire my knowledge only through pain and suffering.

If you have already realized this at a more elementary level of knowledge, it can become a much higher experience once you attain self-mastery—when you reach through the pain experienced as cosmic pain to a neutral experience within the spirit world. You must work through to a point where you live with the *becoming*—the essential nature of all things. This is *intuition* knowledge. Then, however, you are also completely within an experience of knowledge that is no longer bound to the body. As a result, you can return freely to the body and to the material world and live until you die, fully knowing what it means to be *real* in soul and spirit, outside the body.

If you understand this, you also have a picture of what happens when the physical body is abandoned at death and what it means to pass through the gate of death. Having risen to *intuition* knowledge, you already know, through experience, that the soul and spirit enter a world of soul and spirit when the body is abandoned at death. You know what it is to function in a world where one receives no support from the body. Once this knowledge is contained conceptually, you can return to the body. But the important thing is that you learn to live independently of the body—that you learn what happens when you no longer have the use of the body that has been set aside at death, and you enter a world of soul and spirit.

Again, the knowledge that arises from initiation knowledge in relation to immortality is not mere philosophical speculation; it is an experience, or a pre-experience, as it were. You know what you will become. You experience, not the full reality, but an image of reality, which, in a way, corresponds to the whole reality of death. One experiences immortality. Here, too, experience is absorbed to become a part of knowledge.

I have tried to describe how you rise through *imagination* to *inspiration* and *intuition* and, through this, how you eventually become familiar with the whole reality of your being. In the body, you learn to perceive yourself, so long as you remain in that body. The soul and spirit must be freed from the body, after which you become whole for the first time. We come to know only a "limb" of our being through the perceptions of our body and its senses—through the ordinary thinking that results from sensory experience, and is therefore connected to the body, especially the nervous system. We cannot know the whole human being without the will to lift ourselves to ways of knowledge derived from initiation science.

I would like to emphasize again that, once these matters are investigated, anyone who approaches the results with an unbiased mind can understand them with ordinary, healthy reason, just as we can understand what an astronomer or a biologist says about the material world. The results can be tested, and, in fact, you will find that such testing is the first stage of initiation knowledge, which requires an inclination toward truth, since truth is the goal, not inaccuracy and error. Those who follow this path will be able (if destiny allows) to penetrate further and further into the spirit world during earthly life. Today, we must fulfill, at a higher level, the call inscribed above the portal to a Greek temple: "Know yourself." This is not a command to retreat into an inner life, but to investigate the human being—through the body into the being of immortality; through immortal spirit into the unborn; and through the soul into the mediator between earth and spirit. The body can know only the body; the soul can know only the soul; the spirit can know only the spirit. Thus we must look for the active spirit within before we can perceive spirit in the world.

5. General Requirements for Esoteric Development

The requirements that follow must form the basis of esoteric development. If you fail to fulfill these requirements, do not think that you can progress by applying any other means to your inner or outer life. Any meditation, concentration, or other exercises are useless, even harmful, if life is not regulated according to these requirements. Forces cannot be given to you; only those forces already within you can be developed. Those forces do not develop on their own, however, because they are blocked by both outer and inner hindrances. The outer hindrances are decreased through following the following rules of life; the inner hindrances are decreased by special instructions on meditation, concentration, and so on.

The first requirement is that you cultivate absolutely clear thinking. To do this, you must rid yourself of vague, delusive thinking, even if only for a short time each day—at least five minutes, though longer would be better. You must master your thinking. You are not the master if your thoughts and the way you elaborate them are determined by the outer circumstances of work, tradition, social relationships, daily events and activities, your race, and so on. During this brief time, therefore, you must—of your own free will—empty the soul of ordinary, everyday thoughts and, through your own initiative, place a certain thought at the center of your soul. It does not need to be a particularly striking or interesting thought. In fact, it would be better for esoteric development if, to begin with, you choose an uninteresting and insignificant thought. Thinking is thus forced, through its own energy, to become active—and this is the essential—whereas interesting thoughts tend to carry your thinking along with them. It is better if this exercise for controlling your thoughts focuses on a pin rather than Napoleon.

The student begins with the thought, and through inner initiative, associates everything that is pertinent to it. By the end of the exercise period, the thought should be there for the soul just as colorfully and vividly as it was at the beginning. This exercise is repeated each day for at least a month. You may take a new thought every day, but you may also stick with the same thought for several days. At the end of this exercise, you will try to become fully aware of an inner feeling of firmness and security, which is soon noticed if you subtly direct awareness toward your soul. The exercise is concluded by focusing your thinking in the head and middle of the spine, as though you were pouring the feeling of security into that part of the body.

After this exercise has been practiced for about a month, a second exercise should be added. Try to think of something that you would not be likely to do in ordinary life, then make it a duty to perform this action each day. It would be good to choose an action that can be performed every day for as long as possible. It is best to begin with an insignificant act that you must force yourself to do—for example, at a definite time of day, you could water a flower you have purchased. After awhile, a similar act should be added to the first, then a third, and so on—as many as you can without interfering with your other responsibilities.

This exercise, too, should last a month. But, if possible, you should continue the first exercise during this second month, though it is now a less important duty than during the first month. Nevertheless, it must not be forgotten, otherwise you will quickly notice that the fruits of the first month are soon lost, and cluttered, uncontrolled thinking will return. You must take care that, once these fruits are won, they are never lost. When this second exercise has been accomplished, then, with subtle attentiveness, you become aware of feeling an inner impulse of activity in the soul; pour this feeling into the body and let it flow from the head down and around the heart.

In the third month, a new exercise should be placed at the center of your life: you will cultivate equanimity toward the fluctuations of joy and sorrow, pleasure and pain. High feelings of jubilation and depths of despair should be replaced consciously by a mood that lacks noticeable extremes. Be careful that no pleasure carries you away, no sorrow plunges you into the depths, no experience leads you to anger or irritation, no expectation leads to anxiety or fear, no situation leaves you disconcerted, and so on. You need not fear that this exercise will make you life dry and unproductive; rather, you will quickly notice that, by applying this exercise, your moods will be replaced by purer soul qualities. Most important, if you maintain subtle awareness, one day you will discover physical inner tranquility. As in the previous two exercises, you will pour this feeling into the body, allowing it to flow from the heart toward the hands, the feet and, finally, the head. Naturally, you cannot do this after every exercise, because it is not a matter of a single exercise but sustained awareness of your inner soul life. At least once a day, you should evoke this inner tranquility for the soul, and then perform this exercise of pouring it out from the heart. You should maintain a connection with the exercises of the first and second months, just as the second month was connected with the exercise of the first month.

In the fourth month, you should begin a new exercise that is sometimes referred to as developing a positive attitude toward life. In every being, experience, and thing, you always look for the good, the praiseworthy, the beautiful, and so on. This soul quality is best described by a Persian legend of Jesus Christ. One day as Jesus was walking with his disciples, along the roadside they saw a dead dog in an advanced state of decomposition. The disciples all turned away from the repulsive sight; Jesus did not move but looked closely and thoughtfully at the animal, and then he said, "What beautiful teeth this animal has." What the others saw was ugly and repulsive, but Jesus was looking for beauty. This is how an esoteric student tries always to look for the positive in every phenomenon and being. You will soon notice that, behind the mask of something repulsive, there is hidden beauty; behind the mask of a criminal there is hidden goodness, and a divine soul hides behind the mask of a lunatic.

In a certain sense, this exercise is connected with abstaining from criticism. Do not misunderstand this in the sense of calling black "white" or white "black." There is a difference, however, between a judgment that comes from your own personality—colored by your personal sympathy or antipathy—and an attitude that lovingly enters someone or something alien and wonders how that being came to be a certain way. This attitude, by its very nature, tries to help instead of simply finding fault and criticizing.

Here, it is not valid to argue that life circumstances cause people to find fault and condemn. In such cases, circumstances are such that the person in question cannot go through real esoteric training. There are, in fact, numerous life circumstances that prevent a productive esoteric training. In such cases, individuals should not, despite everything, impatiently desire progress that is possible only under certain conditions. If, for one month, you consciously turn your mind toward the positive aspects of all your experiences, you will gradually notice that a feeling is creeping into you, as though your skin were becoming porous all over, and as if your soul were opening wide to all sorts of surrounding subtle processes that previously escaped your notice. The important thing here is that every human being should combat the prevalent lack of attentiveness to such subtleties.

Once you notice that these feelings are expressed in the soul as a kind of bliss, in thought you guide this feeling to the heart, from there into the eyes, and then out into the space all around yourself. You will notice that, in this way, you acquire an intimate relationship to that space. You grow out and beyond yourself, so to speak. You come to think of a part of your surroundings as belonging to you. You will need a great deal of concentration for this exercise, and, above all, you must see that all turbulent feelings, all passions, and all over-exuberance have an absolutely destructive effect on the attitude described. As recommended for the earlier months, you should continue to repeat the previous exercises.

In the fifth month, you should try to cultivate a feeling in yourself that confronts every new experience in a completely unbiased way. Esoteric students must break entirely free from the attitude that, when confronted by something new, says, "That's news to me! I refuse to believe such an illusion." At every moment, you must be prepared to accept something completely new. Nothing you have ever acknowledged as being in accord with natural law and nothing you have considered impossible should hinder your ability to accept a new truth. Although extreme, it is correct that, if an esoteric student were to hear someone say, "Since last night, the church steeple seems to have bowed over," the appropriate response should be an openness to the possibility that one's previous knowledge of natural law may have to be broadened to include such a seemingly unprecedented occurrence.

If you turn your attention, in the fifth month, to developing this mental attitude, you will notice a feeling creeping into your soul, as though something were coming to life and stirring in the space around you. This is an extremely delicate and subtle feeling. You must try to be aware of this delicate vibration in your environment and let it flow, as it were, through all five senses, especially the eyes and the ears, and the skin, to the degree that it involves your sense of warmth. At this stage of esoteric development, you pay less attention to the effects of these stimuli on the senses of taste, smell, and touch. Also at this stage, it is not yet possible to distinguish the numerous harmful influences from the intermingled good influences in this sphere; therefore, you must leave this for a later stage.

In the sixth month, you should try to systematically repeat all five exercises, again and again, alternating them regularly. As a result, a beautiful equilibrium of soul gradually develops. You will especially notice that your previous dissatisfaction with certain phenomena and beings completely disappears. The soul develops an attitude that reconciles all experiences. This mood is not in any way indifferent, but enables you to work, for the first time, toward real progress and improvement in the world. You reach a tranquil understanding of matters that were previously closed to your soul. Your very gestures and bearing are changed by the influence of these exercises, and if, one day, you notice that your handwriting has assumed a new character, you will know that you are about to reach a first rung on the ladder to comprehension.

Two things must again be emphasized. First, these six exercises neutralize the possible harmful influences of other esoteric exercises, so that only their benefits remain. Second, only these exercises can guarantee a positive result of your efforts in meditation and concentration. As an esotericist, you must not be content with fulfilling, however conscientiously, the demands of conventional morality. Such morality can be very egoistic, if you intend to be good just so others will see you as a good person. Esoteric students do not do what is good merely because they want to be thought of as good, but because, little by little, they see that goodness alone promotes evolution, and that evil, stupidity, and ugliness create hindrances to evolution.

You should understand the rules that follow, so that you can arrange your life to include continuous self-observation, self-direction, and, especially, observation of these rules for inner life. Unless such rules are observed, esoteric training, particularly when it rises to higher worlds, will lead students only to disaster and confusion. On the other hand, if you try to live within the spirit of these rules, you need not fear esoteric training. Even if you think you are not following these rules adequately, you need not despair. It is enough if you honestly try to keep sight of these rules in your life. Above all, this honesty must be self-honesty. Many have deceived themselves in this way. Students tell themselves that they will strive in a pure sense. But when they test this, they find much egoism and cunning self-regard hiding in the background. In particular, it is often such feelings that wear a mask of selfless effort and mislead students. You cannot test yourself too often or too seriously by searching for such feelings hidden deep in your soul. If you energetically pursue these rules, you will increasingly free yourself of such feelings.

Rule one: *No unproven idea will enter my consciousness.* Observe the number of ideas, feelings, and will impulses that occupy your soul, acquired through your position in life, your profession, family connections, nationality, the spirit of the time, and so on. Do not assume that ridding the soul of such content would be a moral act for everyone. After all, people gain firmness and security in life because they are supported by their nation, the spirit of the time, family, education, and so on. People would soon find themselves without support in life if they were to carelessly throw these things away. It is especially undesirable for those with weak personalities to go too far in this direction. Esoteric students should be particularly clear that, along with observing this first rule, they must gain a greater understanding of all the actions, thoughts, and feelings of others.

This rule must not lead you to become impulsive or, for example, to attempt a break with everything you were born into or your position in life. On the contrary, the more you test, the more you will see the purpose of everything in your environment. It is not a matter of arrogant rejection or fighting these things; it is a matter of becoming inwardly free of them by carefully testing everything related to your own soul. Then, through your own soul forces, light will flood all of your thoughts and actions, your awareness will be enlarged accordingly, and you will increasingly heed the spiritual laws revealed to your soul. You will no longer blindly follow the world around you.

Of course, since you have to verify everything, you will also want to test the esoteric teachings from your teacher. But such testing must be understood in the right way. You cannot always test something directly; often, you must test indirectly. For example, no one today can prove that Frederick the Great ever lived. One can prove only that the means of communicating accounts of Frederick the Great are trustworthy. Your investigation must begin in the right place. Your faith in so-called authority should be like this. If you are told something that you cannot comprehend directly, it is most important to investigate, on the basis of available material, whether the source is trustworthy, or whether you are being told things that merely evoke a bias and presumption of truth. Thus, you can see the importance of beginning your investigation at the right level.

Rule two: *My soul will observe a living obligation to continually increase the number of my ideas.* For esoteric students, there is nothing worse than wanting to limit one's concepts to those already held and trying to understand everything through them. It is very important to acquire new concepts. If this does not happen, you will be conceptually unprepared when you encounter suprasensory insights. To your disadvantage, or at least to your dissatisfaction, you will be overwhelmed by those insights—dissatisfied because, under such circumstances, you may be surrounded by suprasensory experiences without being the least aware of them. Not a few students may already be surrounded by higher experiences, but they are aware of them because of the poverty of their concepts; they hold completely inaccurate expectations of such experiences. Many people are not at all inclined to laziness in outer life, yet in their conceptual life they are not very likely to enrich themselves with new ideas.

Rule three: *I will regard all knowledge that comes to me—whether positive or negative—without like or dislike.* There was an ancient initiate who always told his students, "You will not come to understand the soul's immortality until you can accept, equally, the ideas that the soul might perish after death, or that it might live eternally. As long as you want to live forever, you cannot conceive of the state after death." This important example applies to all truth. As long as you have the slightest desire for one answer or the other, the pure light of truth will not enlighten you. For example, if, in self-observation, you have even the most secret desire that your good qualities will shine through, this wish becomes an illusion that blocks true self-knowledge.

Rule four: *I must overcome my aversion to the "abstract."* As long as you depend on concepts derived from the sensory world, you cannot reach the truths of higher worlds; you must try to acquire sense-free concepts. Of these four rules, this is the most difficult, especially given the conditions of life today. Materialistic thinking has largely deprived people of an ability to think in sense-free concepts. You must often try to think concepts that, in the outer sensory world, never exist in a perfect way, but only in approximation—for example, a circle. A perfect circle does not exist; it can only be thought. But this conceptual circle is the law behind all circular forms. Or you can think of a high moral ideal, which cannot be completely realized perfectly by anyone. Nevertheless, it is the law behind many human actions.

You will never advance esoterically unless you recognize the full importance in life of so-called abstract thinking and enrich your soul with such concepts.[1]

---

1. For more on these rules, see Rudolf Steiner, *How to Know Higher Worlds*, "Requirements for Esoteric Training."

6. The Great Initiates

It may well be said that the anthroposophic worldview is distinguished from any other by the way it satisfies so well one's desire for knowledge. Today, we often hear that we cannot know certain things, and that our capacity for knowledge has certain limits, beyond which we cannot venture. If you are familiar with modern philosophy, you constantly hear of these limits to knowledge, especially among the schools of philosophy that originated with Immanuel Kant (1724–1804). The understanding of anthroposophists and of those who practice mysticism is distinguished from such doctrines, because it refuses to set limits on our capacity to know, seeing it instead as something to be both widened and uplifted. In a sense, isn't it very arrogant to consider one's capacity for knowledge decisive at its present level, and to deny the capacity to go beyond certain limits of knowledge? An anthroposophist might say, "Today, I have reached a certain point in human knowledge; I know certain things and not others. Nevertheless, I can cultivate my human capacity for knowledge and reach a higher level."

The essential goal of what we call a school of initiation is to raise the human capacity for knowledge to a higher level. It is correct for those at a lower level of knowledge to say that their knowledge is limited and that they cannot know certain things. But we can lift ourselves above that level of knowledge and move on to a higher level, where it is possible to gain knowledge that was impossible at a lower level. This is the essence of initiation, and the purpose of initiation schools is to deepen, or heighten, knowledge. This means lifting ourselves to the level of knowledge made available by our nature, but that we must acquire for ourselves through many years of patient exercise.

In every age there have been such initiation schools. Among every culture and race, those with higher knowledge have come out of the schools of initiation. The essence of such schools is expressed in the initiates who gave the world its various religions and worldviews. And the great initiates themselves soared above the lower levels of human capacities for knowledge and, through the inspirations they received, were acquainted with the highest knowledge available to us in this world.

Today we wish to briefly illuminate the essence of those great initiates. As in every science and spiritual process, we must first learn the method whereby we can penetrate knowledge, and this is also true of initiation schools. Here, too, it is a matter of being led through certain methods to higher levels of knowing, about which we have spoken specifically. I will briefly refer to the relevant stages. Certain stages of knowledge can be attained only in the intimacy of initiation schools, where there are teachers who experienced each school, devoted themselves to every exercise, and truly contemplated each step and every level. We should entrust ourselves only to such teachers of initiation schools.

In those schools, it is true that there is no suggestion of "authority" and dogmatism. The governing principle is based entirely on counsel and giving advice. Those who have gone through a certain level of learning and acquired experiences of the higher, suprasensory life know the inner path to higher knowledge. Only such teachers are qualified to say what we ought to do. It is simply necessary to have trust between student and teacher in this area. Those who lack such trust cannot learn;

those who have it quickly realize that esoteric, mystic, and mystery teachers recommend only what they themselves have gone through. What concerns us is that, looking at the whole human being, it is really only the outer visible aspect of human nature that is complete today. This must become clear to those who wish to become students of the mysteries: as human beings, we are in no way complete; we are in the process of developing so that, in the future, humankind will reach many higher stages.

It is the physical human body that has attained the image of God and arrived at the highest stage in humankind—what we see with our eyes and perceive with our senses. This is not, however, the only thing that human beings possess. We have even higher members of our human nature. To begin with, we have a member we call the ether body. This body can be seen by those who have cultivated their "soul organs." Through the ether body, human beings are not merely a creation in which chemical and physical forces are at work; we are living creations endowed with capacities for growth, life, and propagation. You can see this ether body—a kind of human archetype—if you "suggest away" the ordinary physical body through the art of clairvoyance (which will be described).

You know how, through ordinary hypnotism and suggestion, you can say to someone that there is no lamp here, and that person actually sees no lamp. If you develop a strong enough will in yourself—one that entirely shuts out physical perception—you can, despite seeing a space, completely suggest away that physical space. Then, instead of empty space, you see it filled with a kind of archetype. That archetype has a form similar to the physical body. It does not, however, have the same nature throughout, but is fully organized. It is interlaced with fine veins and streams, and it also has organs. This creation, this ether body, produces our essential life. Its color can be compared only to the color of a young peach blossom. It is not a color in the sun's spectrum, but something like violet tinged with red. This is our second body.

The third body is the aura, which I have often described. It is the cloud-like formation in which the human being is like an egg-shaped cloud.[1] It expresses everything that lives in us as lust, passion, and feeling. Joyful, self-sacrificing feelings are expressed in the aura as luminous streams of color; physical feelings of hate as dark tones of color; focused, logical thoughts as sharp outlines; illogical, confused thinking as figures with blurry outlines. Thus, this aura gives us an image of what lives in a person's soul as feelings, passions, and impulses.

Human beings, as described here, are just as they were when placed on earth—from the "hand of nature"—at approximately the beginning of the Atlantean race.[2] As soon as this fertilization by the eternal spirit took place, human beings appeared with three members: body, soul, and spirit. Today this human three-fold nature assumes a somewhat different form. Since the time when nature released the human being, ever since self-awareness arose, human beings have worked on their own being. This self-development is the refinement of the human aura; it also means sending light into the aura from this self-awareness. Those who are at a very low level of development and have never worked on themselves (the most uncivilized brutes) have the aura that was provided by nature. Those within our civilization and culture, however, generally have auras that they themselves have helped to develop. People develop themselves insofar as they are self-

1. I spoke of this before in my description of the origin of humanity. — RUDOLF STEINER. [See, for example, Rudolf Steiner, *Cosmic Memory: Prehistory of Earth and Man,* chapter 18, "The Fourfold Man of Earth."]
2. I previously described what is meant by the "Atlantean race." — RUDOLF STEINER. [See Rudolf Steiner, *An Outline of Esoteric Science,* pp. 239–252.]

aware, and their efforts are expressed primarily through changes in the human aura. All that people have learned through nature, everything people have taken in since learning to speak and think with self-awareness, is a recent acquisition in the human aura and brought about by their own activity.

Imagine yourself back in the Lemurian age [before the age of Atlantis], in which human beings already had warm blood flowing through their veins for some time. In the middle of that age, they were fertilized with spirit, but they were not yet capable of clear thought. This was at the beginning of evolution, when spirit had only just taken possession of the physical body. At that time, the human aura was still a product of natural forces. One could then perceive, at a certain place inside the head, a smaller, bluish aura, which is still true of people at a very low level of development. This smaller aura is the outer auric expression of the self-awareness. The more we have developed this self-awareness through thought and effort, the more this small aura spreads out over the other, so that they are often completely changed within a short time.

Those who live their lives in outer culture—refined, cultured people—work on their aura in a particular way, as dictated by their culture. We absorb the ordinary knowledge offered in our schools and our life experiences, and they perpetually transform our aura. But this transformation must be continuous if people wish to enter a practice of mysticism. You must make a special effort to develop yourself. Instead of accepting only what culture offers you and incorporating it into your aura, you must exercise an influence over it in a specific, orderly way. This takes place through "meditation." This inner immersion is the first level that a student of initiation must go through.

What is the focus of this meditation? Just try to recall and reflect on the thoughts that you harbor from morning to night, and consider the way these thoughts are influenced by the time and the place in which you live. Consider whether you can hinder your thoughts; ask yourself if you would have those thoughts if you did not happen to be living in Berlin at the beginning of the twentieth century. At the end of the turn of the century, people did not think as people do today. If you consider the ways that the world changed during the past century, you will see that what passes through your soul from morning to night depends on time and place.

The situation is different when we surrender ourselves to thoughts that have an eternal value. Indeed, there are only certain abstract, scientific thoughts—the highest thoughts of mathematics and geometry—that have eternal value. "Two times two equals four" is valid everywhere, at all times. The same is true of geometric axioms. But aside from a certain basic stock of such truths, we may say that the average person has few thoughts that are independent of time and place. Everything that is dependent unites us with the world, and it exerts only a minimal influence on the essence that endures.

Meditation means simply to surrender ourselves to thoughts that have eternal value, by which we consciously lift ourselves beyond time and place. You can find such thoughts in the great religious writings: the Vedas, the Bhagavad Gita, the Gospel of St. John (from the thirteenth chapter to the end), and *The Imitation of Christ*, by Thomas à Kempis (c.1380–1471). You can gain unlimited benefit by living in such writings with patience and perseverance, deepening yourself anew every day and perhaps working for weeks on one single sentence, thinking and feeling it through. Each day, you can draw an eternal truth into your soul—those from the great initiates or inspired individuals—just as one learns each day to know and love a particular child more and more. It fills you with new life. Other significant sayings come from *Light on the Path,* written by Mabel Collins under the guidance of higher powers.[3] Indeed, in the first four sentences there is something that, when patiently applied in the right way, can take hold of the human aura and fill it with new light.[4] One sees this light in the human aura shining and glistening. Bluish shades arise in place of the reddish or reddish-brown shimmering shades, and, in place of yellow, clear reddish colors arise, and so on. The colors of the aura are transformed by the influences of these eternal thoughts. Students do not perceive to begin with, but they gradually begin to notice the deep influence that emanates from a transformed aura.

If, in addition to these meditations, you consciously and scrupulously practice certain virtues, certain soul achievements, your sense organs of the soul will develop within this aura. These are needed for sight into the soul world, just as we need physical sense organs to see into the material world. Nature planted the outer senses into the body, and, likewise, we must, with regularity, plant the higher sense organs of the soul into our aura. Meditation ripens us from within outward, forming, developing, and interweaving the available capacities of the soul's senses.

If you wish to cultivate these sense organs, however, you must turn your attention toward specific soul accomplishments. In the human organization, there is a series of such organs, which we call "lotus flowers." This is because the astral image—which begins to evolve in your aura through the exercises described— assumes a form that recalls a lotus flower. Of course, this is only a likeness, just as one might speak of the "wings" of the lung,

---

3. This early Theosophical work may be found in *Inspirations from Ancient Wisdom.* See also Rudolf Steiner, *From the History and Contents of the First Section of the Esoteric School, 1904–1914,* "Exegesis to *Light on the Path* by Mabel Collins."
4. The four lines are: "Kill out ambition; Kill out desire of life; Kill out desire of comfort; Work as those work who are ambitious."

which merely resemble wings. The two-petaled lotus is found in the middle of the head, just above the nose, between the eyes; the sixteen-petaled lotus flower is near the larynx; the twelve-petaled lotus is in the area of the heart; and the ten-petal lotus is in near the pit of the stomach. Farther down we find the six-petaled and four-petaled lotus flowers. For now, however, I want to discuss only the sixteen-petal and twelve-petal lotus flowers.

In the Buddha's teachings, you are given an account of the "eightfold path." Now, just ask yourselves why the Buddha specifically described the eightfold path as especially important for the attainment of higher levels of self-development. The eightfold path is 1) right resolve, 2) right thinking, 3) right speech, 4) right action, 5) right living, 6) right effort, 7) right memory, and 8) right contemplation (or meditation). What a great initiate such as the Buddha gives does not come from vague ideals, but from knowledge of human nature. He knows how the practice of such soul exercises will affect future development of a body. If we look at the sixteen-petaled lotus in a typical person today, we will see very little. It is, as it were, in the process of flaring up again. In the ancient past, this lotus flower was present, but it has reversed its development. Today it is reappearing, partly because of human cultural activity. In the future, however, the sixteen-petaled lotus will again reach full development. It will glisten vividly with sixteen spokes, or petals, each appearing in a different shade of color; and eventually, it will move to the right. Everyone in the future will possess and experience something that is being cultivated today by all who consciously seek development in a school of initiation, in order to become leaders of humankind. Now, eight of those sixteen petals were formed in the distant past; there are still eight that must be developed if esoteric students want to be able to use these sense organs. They will be developed by those who consciously take the eightfold path with awareness and clarity, those who consciously practice the eight soul activities given by the Buddha, and those who arrange their soul life so as to take hold of themselves and practice the eight virtues as vigorously as possible while sustained by meditation, thus causing the sixteen-petaled lotus to bloom and move toward real perception.

Regarding the twelve-petaled lotus in the region of the heart, six petals were developed in the ancient past, and six must be developed by everyone in the future, and by today's initiates and their students. In every handbook of spiritual science, you can find references to certain virtues, which are the most important ones to be acquired by those aspiring to the level of *chela,* or student. The six virtues you find in every handbook concerned with self-development are 1) control of thinking, 2) control of action, 3) tolerance, 4) steadfastness, 5) impartiality, and 6) equanimity, or what Angelus Silesius calls composure. These virtues (which must be practiced consciously and attentively along with meditation) develop the final six petals of the twelve-petaled lotus.

These six virtues are not gathered arbitrarily, nor are they marked by haphazard, individual inner feelings; they are given from the great initiates' deepest knowing. Initiates recognize that those who really wish to evolve to higher suprasensory levels develop the twelve-petaled lotus. To this end, today they must develop, through these six virtues, the six petals that were left undeveloped in the past. You can see how, essentially, the great initiates gave instructions for life out of deep knowledge of the human being. I could enlarge on these remarks to yet other organs of knowledge and sight, but I want to give you a only brief outline of the initiation process, and these indications should be enough for this.

Once we progress to the degree that the astral sense organs begin to form, when we can perceive not only the sensory impressions in our surroundings but also what belongs to the soul—in other words, when we can see the nature of the human aura as well as that of animals and plants—we begin a completely new stage of instruction. No one can see into the soul's environment before the lotus flowers begin to revolve, just as we can see no color or light without eyes. When this barrier is pierced, however, when we have gone beyond the preliminary levels of knowledge and gain insight into the soul world, we become true students. This takes us through four levels of knowledge.

What happens the moment we pass beyond the first steps and become a chela? We have seen how everything just discussed relates to the astral body. This is organized throughout by the human body. Those who have gone through this development have a totally different aura. When we have illuminated the astral body through self-awareness—when we have become the luminous organization of our astral body—we say that we have illuminated our astral body with *manas*. Manas is simply an astral body ruled by self-awareness. It is the same as the astral body, but at a different level of development.

You must understand what this means before you can practice mysticism according to the seven principles in spiritual scientific handbooks. Everyone acquainted with the mystical path of development, those who know anything about initiation, will tell you that these are valuable for theoretical study, but for mystic practice they are useless unless you understand the relationship between the lower and the higher principles. No practicing mystic recognizes more than four members: the physical body (in which chemical and physical laws are active), the ether body, the astral body, and finally the I, or self-awareness, also called *kama manas* at the present stage of development, the self-aware thinking principle. Manas is simply what the I has worked into the body. The ether body, in its present form, is not influenced by the I. We can influence our growth and nourishment indirectly, but not in the same way that we cause desires, thoughts, and ideas to arise from self-awareness. We cannot directly influence our nourishment, digestion, or growth. In humankind, these have no connection to the I. The ether body must be influenced by the astral body, the so-called aura. To work on the human ether body, the "self" of the astral body must penetrate the ether body, just as a person, as described, works on the astral body, or aura. Then, through meditation, inner immersion, and practicing soul activities (which I have also described), when you reach the point where the astral body has organized itself, then the work extends into the ether body, which receives the "inner word." Then you will not only hear the phenomena around you, but also you will hear within you your ether body and the inner meaning of phenomena.

I have often said that the spiritual essence of phenomena is a reverberation. I have said that, correctly speaking, practicing mystics talk of sound in the spirit world, just as one does of light in the astral, or desire, world. There is a good reason why Goethe says, when guiding *Faust* to heaven:

> The sun sounds, in the ancient way,
> Singing in brother spheres.[5]

Nor are the words of Ariel meaningless as Faust is escorted by the spirits into the spiritual world:

> Thundering for spirit ears
> The new day is already born.[6]

---

5. Raphael: "Die Sonne tönt, nach alten Weise, / In Brudersphären Wettgesang ..." (*Faust,* part 1, "Prologue in Heaven").
6. "Tönend wird für Geistesohren schon der neue Tag geboren" (*Faust,* part 2 "Charming Landscape")

Of course, this inner sound—this inner word, through which things express their nature—is not perceptible at all to the physical ear; it is an experience that you have once you are able to influence the ether body from your astral body. Then you have become a true student of the great initiates, and you can be led further along this path. Once you have ascended this step, you become "homeless," because, essentially, you have discovered the connection with a new world; it rings out to you from the spirit world, and because you are, as it were, no longer at home in this physical world. Do not misunderstand this; students who have reached this stage are still good citizens, family providers, and good friends, just as they were before reaching the level of chela. You need not be torn away from anything. What you experience is an evolution of the soul, thus gaining a new home in a world behind the physical one.

What happens, then? The spirit world sounds within you, and, through this spiritual sound, you overcome illusion—the illusion that deceives all human beings before they begin this stage of development. It is the illusion of a personal self. People believe they are separate personalities, detached from the rest of the world. Simple reflection, however, could teach people that, even physically, we are not independent beings. Bear in mind that, if the temperature in this room were 200 degrees higher than it is now, none of us would survive. If the outer situation were to change in this way, suitable conditions for human physical existence would no longer exist. We are a continuation of the outer world, and the notion of separate beings is absolutely inconceivable. This is even more the case in the worlds of soul and spirit. So you can see that what you think of as a "self" is merely an illusion; you are a part of universal divine spirit. This is where you overcome the personal self—where you understand the mystic chorus of Goethe's *Faust:* "All that passes is only a parable."[7] What we see is merely an image of eternal being. We are only a picture of eternal being. Once we surrender our separate being—the separate life we live through our ether body—we become a part of universal life.

Now one attains what we call *buddhi* as a level of development in the ether body, which no longer maintains a separate existence but joins universal life.[8] Those who have attained this level have reached the second level as a chela, or student. All doubt and reservation fall away from the soul; you can no longer be superstitious or sustain doubt. You no longer have any need to gain truth for the purpose of comparing your views to the world around you, but now live within sound, the "word" of phenomena. The nature of each phenomenon resounds from its being. There is no more superstition, no more doubt. This is called "surrendering of the keys of knowledge to the student." Once you reach this level, word sounds from the spirit world. Your words are no longer an echo of this world, but an echo of what comes from another world and works into this world, but cannot be perceived with our outer senses. Such words are messengers from the Godhead.

When you advance beyond this level, a new one arises. This is attained by those who can directly influence what takes place within the physical body. Previously, your influence extended only to the ether body, but now it extends also to the physical body. Your actions must set the physical body in motion, and what you do is incorporated into something we call *karma*. But people do not work on this consciously; they do not understand how each action leads to a consequence. Now, however, you

---

7. "Alles Vergängliche ist nur ein Gleichnis" (*Faust,* part 2, "Mountain Gorges, Forest, Rock, and Desert").

8. Buddhi (Sanskrit) = intelligence; the passive spiritual vehicle, or latent ideation, of Atma, serving to connect it with manas, the individual self.

begin to act consciously in the physical world, so that you affect your karma consciously. Consequently, through physical actions, you begin to influence your karma.

Now, not only does sound come from the objects around you, but you have reached the level where you can speak the names of all things. The people of our present culture live in such a way that they can speak only one name in reference to themselves: "I." This is the only name people have for the self, although those who immerse themselves in esoteric knowledge arrive at depths that psychology can only dream of. You are the only one who can call yourself by the name "I." No one else can say this to you. We must say "you" to everyone else, and they must say the same. With all of us, there is something to which we can apply the name "I." Because of this, Hebrew mystery teachings speak of an inexpressible name of God. It is a direct proclamation of God in the human being. It was forbidden to speak this name in vain or in a profane way; hence the sacred awe and significance when the Jewish mystery teachers spoke that name. "I" is the one word that says something to you that can never approach you from the outer world. Thus, just as people can call only themselves "I," esoteric students at the third level give all phenomena in the world names that they received from *intuition.* This means that they have entered the universal I; they speak from the universal I. They may call everything by its most profound name, whereas the most people today can say "I" only to themselves. When you have arrived at this stage, you are called a "swan." One who has risen to the point of naming all things is called a swan, the messenger of all things.

What lies beyond these three levels cannot be expressed in ordinary language. It requires knowledge of a special language taught only in mystery schools. The next level is the stage of "the veiled." And beyond that are the stages that belong to the great initiates, those who have always given the great impulses to our cultures. They began as chelas and acquired the keys of knowledge. Next they were led into regions where the universal and the names of things were revealed to them. Then they ascended to the stage of the universal, whereby they had deep experiences that qualified them to establish the great religions of the world.

It was more than the great religions, however, that arose from the great initiates; it was every powerful impulse and all that is important in the world. Consider just two examples, which show the kind of influence exercised in the world by the great initiates who went through esoteric training. Let us go back to ordinary life when students in the initiation schools were guided by Hermes. Ultimately, such guidance consisted of ordinary, so-called esoteric, scientific instruction. I can describe the nature of such instruction only briefly. It was shown how cosmic spirit descended into the physical world, incarnated here, and began a new physical existence, and how he then reached the highest level of humanity and celebrated his resurrection. Paracelsus, in particular, expressed this beautifully: "The individual beings we encounter in the outer world are the individual letters, and the word that is formed from them is 'humanity.'" Outwardly, we have all contributed human virtues or failings to this creation. Humanity, however, is a fusion of all this. Esoteric instruction in the Egyptian mystery schools taught, in detail and with richness of spirit, how the whole macrocosm is fused within humanity as a microcosm.

Later, Hermetic instruction arose. Ordinary understanding can grasp what I just said. But Hermetic instruction can be grasped only by those who have attained the first level of chela. They can learn a special script, which is neither arbitrary nor a matter of chance, but expresses the great laws of the spirit world. This script is not, like ours, made up arbitrarily of fixed, individual letters and parts; it is born out of the spiritual law of nature itself, and those who become versed in this script possess this natural law. Thus, their view of soul and astral space itself is determined by law. What they conceive is imagined in terms of the great signs of that script. They gain the ability to do this once they have renounced the self; they unite with primal, eternal law. Hermetic instruction is now finished. Henceforth, they may be admitted to the first level of an even deeper initiation. At this stage, they should experience something in the astral world, the essential soul world, that has significance beyond the cosmic cycles. Once they have developed the full effect of the astral senses—so that they work right down into the ether body—for three days they are led into a deep mystery of the astral world. In that world, they experience what I have described as the primal origin of earth and humanity. They experience this descent of the spirit, the separation of Sun, Moon, and Earth, and the beginning of humanity—this whole series of phenomena.[9] At the same time, these become a picture before them, after which they emerge. Now that they have this great experience of the mystery school behind them, they go among the people and relate what they experienced in the astral world of soul. And what he relates runs approximately like this:

> Once, there was a divine couple, Osiris and Isis, who were united with the earth. They were regents of everything that happened on earth. Osiris, however, was captured by Typhon and cut into pieces, and Isis had to search for his corpse. She did not bring it home, but distributed graves of Osiris in various parts of the earth. Thus, he was brought completely down to earth and buried here. Then a ray from the spirit world fell on Isis, and fertilized her by immaculate conception with the new Horus.

---

9. Rudolf Steiner describes this process of cosmic evolution in detail in *An Outline of Esoteric Science,* chapter 4.

This image is simply a powerful representation of what we know as the separation of Sun and Moon, and as the dawning of humankind. Isis is the image of Moon; Horus is earthly humankind and earth itself. Before human beings were endowed with warm blood and clothed with a physical body, they experienced powerful images of what had occurred in the soul world. In the beginning of the Lemurian, Atlantean and Arian evolutions, humankind was always prepared by the great initiates to receive the great truths of such pictures. Consequently, those truths were not merely recounted, but given as images of Osiris and Isis. All the great religions that we encounter in antiquity arose from the great initiates' experiences in astral space. The great initiates emerged from those experiences and spoke to each culture in ways they could understand—that is, in pictures of what they had experienced in the mystery schools. This was the situation in ancient times. Only through such a school of initiation could one rise to higher astral experience.

All of this changed with the arrival of Christianity. It cut into evolution with great significance. Since the appearance of Christ, it has been possible for people to become initiates of nature, just as we speak of poets of nature. There have been Christian mystics who, through grace, became initiates. Paul was the first to carry Christianity into the world under the influence of the words, "Blessed are they that have not seen, and yet have believed" (John 20:29). The vision on the road to Damascus was an initiation beyond the mysteries. I cannot go into further detail here.

It was the great initiates who gave the impetus to every great movement and culture. From medieval times, there is a beautiful myth that may be said to show us this at a time when people did not yet require materialistic foundations. This myth arose in Bavaria and thus assumed the garb of Catholicism. Here is what happened: So-called civic culture, or modern citizenship, arose at that time in Europe. The development of humankind and that of each soul to a higher level was understood by mystics as the progress of the soul, or the feminine element in human beings. A mystic sees something feminine in the soul, and this was fertilized by the lower sensory impressions of nature and by eternal truths. In every historical process, a mystic sees this process of fertilization. Those who see deeply into the human path of development—those who see the spiritual forces behind physical appearances—know that the profound impulses for human progress are given by the great initiates. Thus, those with a medieval worldview credited the great initiates with the rise of the soul to higher levels during that new period of culture brought about by the growth of cities. This development of cities was brought about by souls who had made a leap forward in history. And it was an initiate who led that move. All powerful stimuli were ascribed to the great lodge of initiates of the Holy Grail. From there came the great initiates who are invisible to ordinary people. Lohengrin was the initiate who provided civic culture with its impulse in the Middle Ages. He was a missionary of the Holy Grail and the great lodge. Elsa of Brabant represented the soul of the city, the feminine element that was to be fertilized through the great initiate. The mediator is the swan. The swan brought Lohengrin into this physical world. The initiate belongs to a higher world and must not be asked his name. The chela, or swan, has been the mediator of this influence.

I have been able to describe only briefly how this great event has again been symbolized for people in a myth. The great initiates have worked in this way and have included in their teachings what they must make known. All those who founded early human cultures also worked in this way—Hermes in Egypt, Krishna in India, Zarathustra in Persia, and Moses among the

Hebrew people. Orpheus continued the work, then Pythagoras, and finally the ultimate initiate, Jesus, who bore the Christ within him.

I have mentioned only the greatest of initiates. These descriptions try to show their connection with the world. What was described here will remain far from the thinking of many people, but those who are aware of the higher worlds in their souls have always raised their eyes not only to the spiritual world, but also to the leaders of humankind. Only from this perspective could they speak in a way as inspired as that of Goethe. But, also among others, you find hints of the divine spark that brings us to the point to which spiritual science also leads us again. You find this in a young, intelligent German poet and thinker, Novalis, whose life has all the appearance of a blessed memory of some former existence as a great initiate. Those who read his work will notice a breath that guides us to a higher world. There is something in him that contains the magic word, though not expressed as explicitly as usual. Thus he wrote beautiful words about the relationship between our planet and humankind. They convey as much to the lowly and undeveloped as they do to an initiate:

> Humanity is the higher sense of this planet, the nerve that links that body with the higher world, the eye that it raises to the cosmos.[10]

---

10. "Die Menschheit ist der höhere Sinn unseres Planeten, der Nerv, der dieses Glied mit der obern Welt verknüpft, das Auge, was er gen Himmel hebt" ("Treatise of the Light," fragment 2109). Novalis (1772–1801) was born Georg Philipp Friedrich Freiherr (Baron) von Hardenberg, and called Friedrich von Hardenberg. The death in 1797 of his young fiancé, Sophie von Kühn, led him to write *Hymnen an die Nacht* (*Hymns to the Night*), a set of six prose and verse lyrics first published in 1800 in the literary magazine *Athenaeum*. Seven months later, Novalis died of tuberculosis, the disease that had claimed Sophie.

7. The Rosicrucian Spiritual Path

Today, I wish to describe the path of knowledge and its fruits. You already know some of the major points that therefore come into consideration. For those who have already heard me speak of the path of knowledge, or who have read the magazine *Luzifer,* especially issue thirty-two, something new will be offered when we discuss the path of knowledge that occurs only within the intimacy of spiritual scientific circles. The main discussion involves a path of knowledge that can be traced through the Western Rosicrucian spiritual stream, which has invisibly guided European culture spiritually since the fourteenth century.

The Rosicrucian movement worked in complete secrecy until the last third of the nineteenth century. True Rosicrucianism could not be found in books and was not allowed to be discussed publicly. Only in the last thirty years have a few Rosicrucian teachings been made public through the theosophical movement. Before then, it was taught only in the most restricted circles. The most elementary teachings of the Rosicrucians are a part of Theosophy today—but only the most basic. Humankind is allowed, only gradually, to investigate more deeply the wisdom nurtured in European Rosicrucian schools since the end of the fourteenth century.

First, you should understand that we will not consider just one path of knowledge, but three. But do not take this to mean that there are three truths. There is only one truth, just as the view revealed from the peak of a mountain is the same for all who stand there, whereas there are various ways to reach that peak. As you climb, you have a different view at every point. Only at the very top (which you can reach from different sides) will you have a free, complete view from your own perspective. This is how the three paths of knowledge work. There is the Eastern path of yoga, the Christian-Gnostic path, and the Christian-Rosicrucian path. All three lead to a single truth.

There are three different paths, because human nature is different around the world. You can distinguish three types of human nature. It would be illogical to climb a mountain by selecting a remote path instead of the closest one. Likewise, it would be illogical to take a spiritual path other than the one most appropriate for you. There are many muddled ideas about this in the theosophical movement today, which is still developing from its initial level. It is often thought that there is only one path to knowledge—the yoga path. This path is not the only way to knowledge, and, in fact, it is not a propitious path for those of the European civilization.

Those who consider this only from an external point of view can have little insight into what we are speaking of here, because one could easily conclude that human nature seems to differ little in various lands. When those with spiritual power look at the great differences in human types, it is clear that this path may be good for those of the East—even for some in our culture—but it is certainly not appropriate for everyone. There are some (and only a few Europeans) who could follow the Eastern path of yoga. But for most Europeans, it is not practical. It carries with it certain illusions and even the destruction of soul forces. Eastern and Western natures, though they do not seem so different to modern science, are completely different. An Eastern brain, imagination, or heart works in a completely different way than do the organs of Westerners. What we expect of someone who grew up in Eastern circumstances should not be expected of a Westerner. Those who believe that climate, religion, and society have no influence on the human spirit may also think that the external circumstances of spiritual training make no difference. Those who know the deep spiritual influences that these outer circumstances exert on human nature, however, also understand that the yoga path is not possible for those who remain in a European culture, and that only those few who fundamentally detach themselves from Europe can take that path.

Those who are still inwardly upright and honest Christians, who are permeated with certain principle themes of Christianity, may choose the Christian-Gnostic path, which differs little from the Cabalistic path. For Europeans in general, however, the Rosicrucian path is the proper one. The European Rosicrucian path will be discussed today, as well as the various practices it prescribes and the fruits for those who follow it. No one should think that this path is only for those trained in science or for scholars. The simplest person can take this path. If you do take this path, however, you will quickly be able to counter every argument that can be made against esotericism by European science. This was one of the main purposes of Rosicrucian masters: to arm those who take this path to defend esoteric knowledge. Simple people who entertain only a few popular ideas about modern science, or even none at all, but who have an honest desire for truth, can pursue the Rosicrucian path along with trained scientists and scholars.

There are great distinctions among these three paths of knowledge. The most important one is in the relationship between the student and the esoteric teacher, who gradually becomes a guru or mediates the relationship to a guru. A characteristic of the Eastern yoga schools is that this relationship is very strict. The guru is an unconditional authority over the student. If this were not the case, the training would not have the proper results. Yoga training is impossible without a strong submission to the guru's authority. The Christian-Gnostic, or Cabalistic, path allows a looser relationship with the guru on the physical level. The guru, as the mediator, leads the student to Jesus Christ. On the Rosicrucian path, the guru becomes more and more a friend, whose authority is based on inner agreement. The only possible relationship is one of strong personal trust. Should the slightest mistrust arise between teacher and student, the essential bond would be torn apart, and the forces at play between teacher and student would cease to be effective.

It is easy for students to form false ideas about the role of the teacher. The student might feel a need to speak to the teacher now and then, or that the teacher should remain nearby physically. Certainly, there is an occasional need for a teacher to physically approach the student, but, contrary to the student's belief, this is seldom the case. The effect that a teacher exercises on the student cannot be judged correctly at the beginning of their relationship. A teacher's methods may only gradually reveal themselves to the student. Many words that a student perceives to be spoken by chance are, in fact, very important. They may work subconsciously in the soul, as a beneficial force, to lead and guide. If a teacher exercises such esoteric influences correctly, the real bond will be there with the student. In addition, the forces of loving participation work at a distance, forces that are always at the teacher's disposal and that, later, are gradually revealed to a student who finds the way into the higher worlds. Absolute trust, however, must be unconditional; otherwise it is better to dissolve the bond between teacher and student.

The various precepts that play a role in the Rosicrucian training should be mentioned briefly. These do not need to be encountered in same sequence as given here. According to the character, occupation, and age of a student, the teacher will have to extract this or that from the various spheres, and rearrange them. Only an overview will be given here.

Something very important to the Rosicrucian training is not generally stressed sufficiently in esoteric training. It is the cultivation of clear, logical thinking, or at least working toward this goal. Confused and opinionated thinking must be eliminated immediately. You must become accustomed to viewing the relationships in the world with a broad and unselfish mind. The best exercise for those who wish to take the Rosicrucian path's unpretentious way is the study of the basic teachings of spiritual science. It is not valid to argue that, if you cannot see and verify these things for yourself, it is useless to learn about the higher worlds, the various races and cultures, or reincarnation and karma. This is not valid, because thinking about these truths purifies and disciplines your thinking, so that you are ripened for further measures on the esoteric path. Mostly, people think without bringing order to their thoughts. Thinking is ordered by the guiding principles and periods of human development and planetary evolution and by the broad views opened by the initiates. This is all part of Rosicrucian training; it is called "the study." A teacher, therefore, will suggest that students think deeply about the basic teachings of reincarnation and karma, the three worlds, the akashic record, and earthly and human evolution. The range of basic spiritual science, as it is diffused in modern times, is the best preparation for simpler people.

Those who wish to cultivate even sharper thinking and develop their souls more rigorously should study books written especially for the discipline of one's thinking. Two books were written for just this purpose—in them there is no mention of the word *theosophy*. They are *Truth and Knowledge: Introduction* to *"Philosophy of Spiritual Activity"* and *Intuitive Thinking As a Spiritual Path: A Philosophy of Freedom.* One writes such books with a specific purpose in mind. Those who have a foundation in the intensive training of logical thinking and wish to study more broadly would do well to submit their spirits at once to the "gymnastics for soul and spirit" as required by these two books. This makes them a foundation for Rosicrucian study.

When we observe the physical plane, we receive certain sensory impressions—colors, light, warmth, cold, smells, and tastes, as well as impressions through the senses of hearing and touch. We connect all of these with our intellect and thought activity. These activities belong to the physical plane. You can perceive all of this on the physical plane, but perceptions on the astral level appear completely different. Perceptions are again entirely different on the level of devachan, not to mention in even higher spirit regions.[1] The person who has not yet acquired a glimpse into the higher worlds can still try to imagine them. I am also trying to give you a view of these worlds through images in my current way of representation. Those who ascend to the higher regions see for themselves how they work on them. On every plane, one has new experiences. But one experience remains the same through all worlds up to devachan—one that never changes: it is trained, logical thinking. Once on the buddhi level, this thinking no longer has the same value as it does on the physical plane. Another form of thinking must now come into play. For the three worlds below the buddhi plane, however— the physical, astral, and devachanic planes—the same form of thinking is valid. Therefore, those who train themselves in

---

1. Devachan (Sanskrit) means literally "dwelling of the gods." A state intermediately between two earth lives, into which the I (atma, buddhi, and manas together) enters after its separation from *kama rupa* (desire body), and the disintegration of the lower principles on earth.

orderly thinking through this study in the physical plane will find that such thinking is a good guide in the higher worlds. You will not falter so easily as one who tries to enter the spirit realms with confused thinking. Rosicrucian training thus advises people to discipline their thinking so they can move freely within the higher worlds. When you reach into these higher worlds, you learn new ways of perception, which were not available on the physical plane, but you can master these with your thinking.

The second thing you must learn on the Rosicrucian path of knowledge is *imagination.* You prepare for this by gradually immersing yourself in pictorial concepts that represent the higher worlds in the sense of Goethe's words, "All that passes is only a parable." People generally go through the physical world, taking things as they appear to the senses, not seeing what lies behind. People are pulled down into the physical world as if by a dead weight. We become independent of the physical world only when we learn to view phenomena as symbolic. Consequently, we must try to acquire a "moral" relationship to them. A teacher can provide much guidance in learning to view outer appearances as symbols of the spirit, but students can also do a great deal for themselves. For example, look closely at a meadow saffron and a violet. When I view a meadow saffron as a symbol of melancholy, I regard it not only as it meets me externally, but also symbolizing of a certain quality. In the violet, one can behold a symbol for calm innocence. You can go from object to object, plant to plant, animal to animal and look at them as symbols of spirit. In this way, you make your imaginative capacities more fluid, releasing them from the sharp contours of sensory perception. In each species of animal, you come to see a symbol for a characteristic quality. You perceive one animal as a symbol of strength, another slyness. We must try to pursue such things, not fleetingly, but earnestly and in stages.

Essentially, all human language is spoken symbols. Language is nothing but a speaking in symbols. Every word is a symbol. Even science, which claims to view everything objectively, must use language, and its words work symbolically. If you speak of the wings of lungs, you know that there are really no wings, yet you like the reference. Those who wish to keep their feet on the ground should not lose themselves too much in symbols, but advanced esoteric students will not lose themselves. If you investigate, you will perceive the primordial basis of human language. Deep individuals such as Paracelsus and Jakob Böhme owed much of their development to the opportunities they had (and did not shun) for studying the imaginative significance of language, through conversations with vagrants and farmers. Words such as *nature, soul,* and *spirit* worked completely differently—more strongly. Out in the country, when a farmer's wife plucks the goose's feathers, she calls the inside of the feather "the soul."

Students must discover such linguistic symbols for themselves. In this way, you can loosen yourself from the physical world and learn to lift yourself into the realm of *imagination.* If the world is viewed as a likeness of the human being, it has a powerful effect. If you practice this for a long time, you will notice corresponding effects. When observing a flower, for example, something gradually loosens from the flower. The color, which once clung to the surface of the blossom, ascends like a small flame, hovering freely in space. *Imagination* knowledge forms from such things. It is as if the surfaces of phenomena come loose. The whole space fills with colors—flames hovering in space. Thus, the whole world of light seems to detach itself from physical reality. When a color picture detaches itself and hovers in space, it soon begins to adhere to something. It presses toward something. It does not just stand still; it encloses a being, which now appears in the color as spiritual being. The color that the student has detached from the objects of the physical world clothes the spiritual beings of astral space.

This is where the counsel of the esoteric teacher must intervene, because now the student could very easily go astray. This might happen for two reasons. First, each student must go through a specific experience. The images that are peeled from physical objects (not just colors, but also aural and olfactory sensations) may present themselves in strange, hideous, or even beautiful forms—as animal heads, plant forms, or horrible human faces. This first experience represents a reflection of the student's soul. Particular passions and desires, the evils that remain in the soul, appear to the advancing student as in a mirror in astral space. Now one needs the counsel of an esoteric teacher, who can explain that this is not objective reality, but a reflection of the student's inner being.

You can understand just how much a student must depend on the teacher's advice when you understand the way such images appear. It is frequently emphasized that everything is reversed in astral space and appears as a reflection. For this reason, one can easily be misled by illusions, especially by a reflection of one's own being. The reflection of a passion does not appear only as an approaching animal, which would be manageable, but there is something else you must deal with. Imagine a man who has hidden his evil passions. The reflection of such desires or lust frequently appears as an alluring form, whereas a benevolent characteristic may not appear alluring at all. Again, we are talking about something that was portrayed wonderfully in an ancient saga. You find this image in the legend of Hercules. As he goes on his way, good and evil characteristics confront him. Vices are clothed in the enticing forms of beauty, while virtues are dressed in a more chaste way.

There are yet other hindrances to the student's progress. Even when your are able to see things objectively, there is yet another possibility. Your inner will may be directing and influencing these phenomena as an outer force. You must then bring yourself to a point where you can see through it and understand the strong influence that desire exerts on the astral plane. Everything that has a directing force in the physical world ceases to exist when you arrive in the imaginative world. If, on the physical plane, you imagine that to have done something you really did not do, the physical facts will quickly persuade you that this is not so. This is not true of astral space, where images of your wishes deceive you, and then you need wise guidance to understand how those imaginative images work and to see their true meaning.

The third task of the Rosicrucian training is to learn the occult script. What is this script? There are certain images, or symbols, that are formed by simple lines or by joining colors. Such symbols constitute an occult language of signs. For example, there is a certain process in the higher worlds that functions in the physical world as well—the rotation of a vortex. You can observe this when you look at a star cluster, such as in the constellation of Orion. There you see a spiral, but it is on a physical level. But you can also see this on every other plane. It may present itself as one vortex entwining with another. This figure is found on the astral plane in every possible form. If you understand this figure, you can understand how one race transforms itself into another. At the time when the first sub-race of the current main race formed, the sun was in the sign of Cancer.[2] At

---

2. Root races are the main sequential divisions of life waves on a planetary globe, each lasting millions of years; current humanity comprises the fifth of seven great root races. Root races are each further divided into "sub-races." See *Cosmic Memory: Prehistory of Earth and Man,* chapter 17, "The Life of Earth."

that time, one race entwined with the other, and, because of this, one has this occult sign for Cancer. All of the signs of the Zodiac are occult signs. One just needs to learn and understand what they mean.

The pentagram is also such a sign, to which you learn to connect certain sensations and feelings; it is a counterpart to astral processes. This language of signs, learned as esoteric script, simply reproduces the laws of the higher worlds. The pentagram expresses various meanings. Just as the letter *b* is used in many different words, so a symbol in an esoteric script can have diverse meanings. The pentagram, hexagram, right angle, and other figures may be combined into an occult script that acts as a signpost in the higher worlds. The pentagram represents the fivefold human organization, secrecy, and what lives behind the species soul of roses. If you connect the petals in an image of a rose, you will see a pentagram. Just as the letter *b* means something different in various words, similarly the signs of an occult script also have various meanings, but you must learn to arrange them in the correct way. They are the signposts on the astral plane.

Those who learn to read the occult script and those who see only the individual symbols may be compared to literate and illiterate people in the physical world. Symbols for the script of the physical world are mostly arbitrary. Originally, however, they were like the astral language of signs. Consider an ancient astral symbol, Mercury's staff and the snake. It became the letter *e* in our system of writing. Or look at the letter *w*, which depicts a wave movement of water. It is the soul sign of the human being and at the same time a symbol for *the Word*. The letter *m* is simply an imitation of the upper lip. In the course of evolution, these have all become increasingly arbitrary. At an esoteric level, on the other hand, necessity is the rule. There one is able to live these things.

The fourth step is the so-called rhythm of life. People know very little of such rhythms in daily life, living carelessly and ego-istically. At best, for schoolchildren the lessons carry a certain life rhythm, since the sequence of daily lessons is repeated each week. But who does this in normal life? Nevertheless, you can-not ascend to a higher development without bringing rhythm and repetition into your life. Rhythm rules all of nature—the revolutions of planets around the sun, the annual appearance and withering of plants, and animals and their sexual life. Only human beings are allowed to live without rhythm, so that they can become free. However, they must, of their own accord, bring rhythm back into the chaos. You can establish a good rhythm by practicing esoteric exercises each day at a specific time. You should practice meditation and concentration exer-cises each day at the same time, just as the sun sends its forces to earth at the same time each spring. This is a way to bring rhythm into life. Another is for the esoteric teacher to bring the proper rhythm to the student's breathing. Each day, you spend a short time with the rhythm of inhaling, holding your breath, and exhaling, as determined by the teacher's experience. Thus, through human effort, a new rhythm replaces the old. Bringing rhythm into life in such ways is required for ascending to higher worlds. But no one can do this without a teacher's guidance. It should be brought to awareness here only as a principle.

The fifth step is to learn the correspondence between micro-cosm and macrocosm. Here, a teacher shows how to concentrate your thoughts on certain parts of the body. Some may have heard me speak on the relationship between the senses and the higher worlds.[3] You will recall that the whole cosmos participated in the

---

3. See, for example, Rudolf Steiner, *Founding a Science of the Spirit* (14 lectures, Stuttgart, Aug. 22–Sept. 4, 1906), especially lectures 12–14.

formation of the physical human body. The eye was created by light, by the spirits who work in light. Every point of the physical body is connected with a particular cosmic force.

Consider the point at the top of your nose. At one time, the etheric head protruded way beyond the physical body. Even during Atlantean times, the forehead was a point at which the etheric head went far out beyond the physical head, which is still true of horses and some other animals; in horses, the etheric head still protrudes beyond the physical. In modern human beings, this point in the etheric head is now protected by the physical head, which gives us the ability to develop those parts of the physical brain that enable us to call ourselves "I." This organ is related to a specific process that occurred during the Atlantean development of earth. Esoteric teachers today instruct their students to direct their thoughts and concentrate them at this point. They then give them a mantra, and this stimulates a certain force in this area of the head that corresponds to a certain macrocosmic process, thus evoking a correspondence between microcosm and macrocosm. Through similar concentration on the eye, you acquire knowledge of the Sun. You can find the entire spiritual organization of the macrocosm spiritually within your own organs.

When you have practiced this long enough, you may move on and immerse yourself in what you have thus discovered [the sixth step]. For example, you might search the akashic record for the time during the Atlantean era when the top of the nose reached the condition upon which you have concentrated. Or you find the sun by concentrating on the eye. This sixth step— immersing yourself in the macrocosm—is contemplation. It brings you cosmic knowledge, and through this you expand self-knowledge beyond the personality. This is different from the much loved chatter about self-knowledge. You do not find the self by looking within, but by looking outside. This is the self that produced the eye that was evoked by the sun. When you want to find the aspect of the self that corresponds to the eye, then you must look for it in the sun. You must learn to perceive your self as what lies beyond you. Looking only within yourself leads to a hardening within you and greater egoism. When people claim that they simply need to "let the self speak," they have no idea of the danger involved. Self-knowledge may be practiced only when students of the white path have bound themselves to self-renunciation. Once you have learned to say to everything, "That is I" [or "That is you," *Tat tvam asi*], you are ripe for self-knowledge, as expressed by Goethe in the words of Faust:

> You lead the lot of those alive
> Before me, introducing my kindred
> Among quiet shrubs, in knowing air and water.

All around are parts of our self. This is represented, for example, in the myth of Dionysius, which is why Rosicrucian training places great value on objective, quiet contemplation of the external world. If you want to know yourself, look at yourself in the mirror of the outer world and its beings. Whatever is within your soul will speak to you far more clearly from the eyes of companions than it will if you harden yourself and sink back into your soul. This is an important and essential truth that cannot be ignored by those who wish to take the white path. There are many today who have transformed their ordinary egoism into a more refined egoism. Some call it "theosophical development" when they have allowed the ordinary, everyday self to rise as high as possible. They merely bring out the personal element. True esoteric knowledge, by contrast, shows us how our inner nature is illuminated when we learn to perceive our higher self in the world.

Once you have developed yourself by contemplating these truths, your self flows out into everything. You realize your higher self when you can feel a blossom growing, just as you feel your finger move, and when you know that the whole world is your body. Then you can speak to a flower as you might to a member of your own body: "You belong to me, you are part of me."

Gradually you begin to experience "Godliness," which is called the seventh step of the Rosicrucian path. This element of feeling is necessary to lead you into the higher worlds, where you cannot merely think about higher worlds, but learn to "feel" in them. Thus, you will be shown the fruits of your efforts to learn (under the continued guidance of a teacher), and you need not be afraid that your esoteric path will lead you into an abyss. Everything described as the dangers of esoteric development will not become an issue if you have been guided correctly. If this is the case, the esoteric seeker can truly help humanity.

In *imagination*, the possibility arises for one to go through a certain portion of the night in a state of awareness. Your physical body sleeps as usual, but part of your sleep state becomes animated by meaningful dreams. These are the first indication of your entry into higher worlds. Gradually, you guide your experiences into ordinary consciousness. You begin to see astral beings in your whole environment, even in this room, between chairs, or out in the woods and meadows.

You attain three levels in *imagination* knowledge. At the first level, you perceive the beings behind physical sensory impressions. Behind red or blue there is a being, or behind each rose. Behind each animal is a species, or group soul. You become clairvoyant in the daytime. If you wait awhile and quietly practice *imagination*, steeping yourself in the esoteric script, you also becomes clairaudient in the daytime. At the third level, you learn about everything in the astral world that pulls people down and leads them into evil—but are, in fact, intended to lead people upward. You come to know *kamaloca*.[4]

You attain three further levels through the fourth, fifth, and sixth levels of Rosicrucian training—rhythmic life, understanding the relationship between microcosm and macrocosm, and contemplating the macrocosm. In the first, you gain knowledge of the conditions of life between death and a new birth. This confronts you in devachan. Next is the ability to see how forms are transformed from one state to another. For example, human beings did not always have the lungs they have today; these were acquired during Lemurian times. During the preceding Hyperborean epoch, they had a different form and, before that, another form, because they existed in an astral state. And before that there was another form, because they were in devachan. You could say that, at this stage, you come to know the relationships between the various spheres—that is, you experience how one sphere, or state of form, changes into a different one. In the final step, before entering even higher worlds, you witness the metamorphosis of life conditions. You perceive the way various beings pass through different kingdoms, or "rounds," and how one kingdom become another. You must then ascend to even higher levels, which cannot be discussed further here.

What we have discussed here is enough for you to ponder for now. And these matters must be truly thought through; this is the first step to the heights. Consequently, it is good to have the path laid out once in an orderly way. You may be able to take a

---

4. Kamaloka (Sanskrit) is the semi-material plane, ordinarily subjective and invisible, in which the disembodied "personalities", the astral forms, called *kamarupa* stay until they fade out from it through the complete exhaustion of the effects of the mental impulses that created the phantoms of human and animal passions and desires. It is the Hades of ancient Greeks.

journey in the physical without a map of the country. On the astral level, however, you must have a map. Consider these comments as a kind of map, and they will help you not only in this life, but also when you step through the portal into higher worlds. Those who take up these things through spiritual science will be well served by this map after death. Esotericists know how miserable it can be for those who arrive on the other side with no idea of where they are or what is happening. If you have lived with these teachings of spiritual science, you will know your way around; you will be able to picture these things to yourself. If you do not shrink from taking the path of knowledge, you will gain great benefit for the other world.

8. Imagination Knowledge and Artistic Imagination

Among an esoteric teacher's instructions, *imagination* was the second one named. This means that you do not go through life in the usual way, but with the view behind Goethe's saying, "All that passes is only a parable." Behind every animal and every plant, there is something that should appear to you. In meadow saffron, for example, you will discover an image of the soul's melancholy; in a violet, calm piety; or in a sunflower, strong and vigorous life, self-reliance, and ambition. When you live in this way, you lift yourself to *imagination* knowledge. Then you see a kind of "cool flame" arising from a plant, a color image that leads you into the astral plane. Thus, you are guided to see that things reveal spirit beings from other worlds. It has already been said, however, that you must strictly follow an esoteric teacher, because this is the only way you can distinguish the subjective from the objective. Esoteric teachers can give you the needed stability to continuously correct errors, which is given naturally by the sensory realm. In the astral world, you are easily deceived, and you need the support of someone with experience.

Your teacher gives you a series of instructions when you begin the Rosicrucian path. First, you are given exact instruction as you begin to develop *imagination*. You are told to begin by working to develop a living feeling for whole animal groups—rather than loving an individual animal, or forming a special relationship and experiencing this or that with a particular animal. This will give you an idea of what a group soul is. The individual souls of human beings are on the physical plane, whereas the souls of animals are on the astral plane. Animals do not have a self, or I, on the physical plane.

People often ask whether animals have souls like those of human beings. An animal does have such a soul, but it exists on the astral plane. A single animal is related to the animal-soul just as an individual human organ is related to the human soul. If a finger is painful, the soul experiences it. The sensations of a single organ passes to the soul. This is also true of a group of animals. Whatever happens to a single animal is experienced by the group soul. Consider various lions, for example. A lion's experiences all lead to a common soul. All lions have a common group soul on the astral plane, as do all animal species. If one inflicts pain on a single lion, or if it experiences pleasure, this is passed on to the astral plane, just as the pain of a finger is passed on to the human soul. You can lift yourself to comprehension of the group soul if you can imagine a form that contains all individual lions, just as any general concept contains the individual images belonging to it.

Plants have their soul in the rupa region of the devachan. By learning to survey a group of plants and gaining a definite relationship to their group soul, you learn to penetrate through to the group souls of plants on the rupa plane. When a lily or a tulip is no longer individually special you—when the individuals plants come together into living, densified imaginations and pictures—you will experience something new. The important thing is that this forms a concrete picture in the imagination. Then you will experience the plants that cover the earth—a meadow strewn with flowers—as something completely new; the flowers become a living manifestation of the earth's spirit. It is a manifestation of the various group souls of plants. Just as human tears express an inner sadness of the soul, and just as one's physiognomy expresses the soul, you learn to see the green of plants covering the earth as an expression of the inner processes of the earth's spiritual life. Certain plants thus appear to you as the earth's tears, expressing the earth's inner grief. A fresh *imagination* pours into your soul, just as someone may tremble and be moved by the tears of a friend.

You must go through such moods. And if you endure such a mood in relation to the animal world, you can lift yourself into the astral plane. If you immerses yourself in a mood of the plant world, you raise yourself into the lower region of the devachan plane. Then you see the "flames" that rise from plants; the plants that cover the earth become veiled by a sum of images—the incarnations of light rays that set upon the plants.

You can also approach a dead stone in this way. You can find a fundamental experience in the mineral world. Consider a crystal, glittering with light. When you look at it, you tell yourself that, in a way, it represents physical matter. But there is also a future perspective, to which the esoteric teacher leads a student. People today are still imbued with instincts, desires, and passions. These saturate the physical nature, but an ideal confronts an esotericist: The animal nature of human beings will gradually become refined and purified, to the point where the human body can become just as pure and free of desire as a mineral, which has no craving or desire in response to the surrounding world. The inner material nature of a mineral is chaste and pure. This chastity and purity is the experience that must permeate your being when you observe the mineral world. These feelings vary, since the mineral world manifests in various forms and colors, but the fundamental experience that permeates the mineral kingdom is chastity.

Today, our earth has a very special configuration and form. Let us go back in the earth's evolution. At one time, it had a completely different form. As we immerse ourselves in Atlantis and even further back, we come to increasingly higher temperatures; metals were able to flow as water does today. Today, the metals are veins in the earth, because they once flowed along in streams. Just as lead is hard today and mercury is liquid, lead used to flow, and mercury will eventually become solid. Thus the earth changes, and humankind has always participated in this evolution. In those ages, a physical human being did not yet exist. However, the ether body and astral body were present and could live in those higher temperatures. Sheaths gradually formed and enveloped human beings as the earth cooled.

Something new was always being formed in human beings during earthly evolution, and something equally new was also formed in outer nature. The rudiments of the human eye first arose during the Sun stage of cosmic evolution. First, the ether body formed, and this formed the physical human eye. Just as ice is frozen water, our physical organs were formed from the finer ether body. Physical organs were formed in human beings, while the earth outside became solid. In every age, a human organ formed in conjunction with the formation of a particular configuration in nature. In human beings, the eye was formed; in the mineral kingdom, peridot, or chrysolite, was formed. Thus, you can say that the forces behind the formation of peridot in outer nature also formed the eye in human beings.

When considering any case, it is not enough to say that the human being is a microcosm and the universe is the macrocosm. Esotericism demonstrates the true relationship between humankind and the world. When the physical organ for reasoning was formed during the Atlantean era, lead changed from a fluid to a solid. The same forces ruled both the solidification of lead and the formation of the human organ of intelligence. You cannot understand the human being unless you recognize the connections between humankind and natural forces.

In the socialist movement, there is a group that has distinguished itself by its moderation, and it is the temperate ones who have always retained a good portion of their reasoning faculties. This moderate socialist group is made up of printers, because they have to work with lead. The tariff union between workers and employer was first worked out among the printers. Lead brings about this frame of mind when taken in very small quantities. Another case can be cited in which, similarly, one sees the effects of a metal on a human being. A man began to notice how easily he could find analogies in everything possible. One could conclude that he had been involved with copper, and this turned out to be the case. He played trumpet in an orchestra and, thus, handled an instrument made mostly of copper.

Someday, when the relationship between the outer lifeless world and the human organism has been studied sufficiently, it will be discovered that there is a relationship between people and the surrounding world in many different ways. For instance, there are relationships between the senses and precious stones, some of which are based on the evolution of the senses. We have already seen a relationship between the eye and the peridot. There is also a relationship between onyx and the organ of hearing. Onyx has a remarkable relationship to the oscillations of the human I-being, and esotericists have always seen this. It represents, for example, the life that departs at death. Thus, in Goethe's fairy tale, the dead dog is changed into onyx by the old man's lamp.[1] This intuition of Goethe contains the results of

---

1. "The Fairy Tale of the Green Snake and the Beautiful Lily" (1795). See Paul Allen and Joan DeRis Allen, *The Time Is at Hand!,* which contains a complete translation and discussion of the fairy tale.

esoteric knowledge, and in it we see the relationship between onyx and hearing. Another esoteric relationship exists between the organ of taste and topaz, the sense of smell and jasper, the the sense of warmth and carnelian, and the power of imagination and carbuncle. Carbuncle was the symbol of a productive imagination, which arose in humankind when the carbuncle developed in nature.

German literature mentions that instinctive intuition regarding mineral forces is displayed by poets who were miners—for example Novalis, who studied mining engineering. Kerning chose miners as his esoteric personalities. There is also the poet, Ernst Theodor Amadeus Hoffman, a remarkable spirit who occasionally immersed himself artistically in the secrets of nature, particularly in his tale, "The Mines of Falun." In it, one feels echoes of the esoteric relationships between the mineral kingdom and humankind, and much, too, that shows how spiritual forces take hold of artistic imagination in a remarkable way. Esoteric symbols are drawn deep from real wisdom, and if you penetrate esoteric symbolism, you find genuine knowledge. If you understand the significance of a mineral, you find a way into the upper region of the devachan. When you see a precious stone and become permeated by the feeling of what it says, you find entry to the arupa regions of devachan. Thus, your view widens as more and more worlds dawn. You must not be satisfied with a general indication, but slowly find a way into the whole world.

The mystery center is the essential birthplace of art. In the astral realm, the mysteries were concrete and alive; one could find a synthesis of truth, beauty, and goodness. This was also true of the Egyptian and Asian mysteries, and especially the Eleusinian Greek mysteries. Students there actually saw how spiritual powers submerged themselves in the various forms of existence. At that time, the only science was what people beheld in this way. The only goodness arose in the soul as one gazed into the mysteries. And the only beauty was seen as the gods descended.

We live in a barbaric time, a chaotic age devoid of style. All great ages of art arose from the deepest life of spirit. If you observe the images of Greek gods, you clearly see three distinct types. First, there is the Zeus type, to which Athena and Apollo belong. In these, the Greeks pictured their own race. There was a definite shape in the oval of the eye, the nose, the mouth. Second, we see a group that may be called the Mercury type. The ears and nose are completely different, the hair is woolly and curly. And third, there is the Satyr type, in which we find a completely different form of mouth, a different nose, eyes, and so on. These three types are clearly formed in Greek sculpture. The Satyr type represents an ancient race, the Mercury type the race that followed, and the Zeus type, the fifth race.

In the earlier times, the spiritual worldview permeated everything. During the Middle Ages, this was expressed in crafts; every door latch was a work of art. In outer culture, people still encountered what the soul had created. The modern age is entirely different; it has produced only one style—the warehouse. The warehouse will be characteristic of our time, just as the Gothic buildings—Köln Cathedral, for example—exemplify the Middle Ages during the thirteenth and fourteenth centuries. The cultural history of the future will have to deal with the warehouse, as we look back to the Gothic buildings of the Middle Ages. New life is expressed in these forms. The world will again fill with spirituality through the diffusion of spiritual scientific teachings. Later on, when spiritual life is again expressed in outer forms, we will have a style that expresses that spiritual life. Spiritual science must express itself in externally. Thus, we must see the mission of spiritual science as a cultural mission.

9. Three Decisions on the Path of Imagination Knowledge: Loneliness, Fear, and Dread

We will begin by thinking of those in the midst of today's events [of World War I]:

> Spirits, always watching,
> Guardians of your souls,
> May your wings bring
> To those of Earth
> Committed to your charge
> Our souls' imploring love,
> So that, together with your power,
> Our prayer may flow with aid
> To the souls it seeks in love.

And for those who, because of those events, have gone through the portal of death:

> Spirits, always watching,
> Guardians of your souls,
> May your wings bring
> To those of heavenly spheres
> Committed to your charge
> Our souls' imploring love,
> So that, together with your power,
> Our prayer may flow with aid
> To the souls it seeks in love.

And may the spirit we seek through spiritual knowledge be with you and your hard tasks—the spirit who, for the salvation of earth and the freedom and progress of humanity, passed through the Mystery of Golgotha.

A week ago, we considered souls closely related to us, who, to find them now, must be looked for in spirit worlds. Things were said about those souls that illuminate the whereabouts of beings in the spiritual world. I suggest that we direct our study toward the spiritual path that the human soul can take while still in the body, so that we can find the spiritual realms we spoke of as the dwelling place of the so-called dead. It must be emphasized again and again that the spiritual path appropriate for today requires manifold preparations. Some of this is difficult, but it is necessary. Today I wish to point out certain matters related to the path of knowledge from the perspective of what may be called *imagination* knowledge.

It is very familiar to you, my dear friends, that the human soul cannot have experiences in the spiritual world unless it is free of the physical body. Through the body, we gain only experiences of physical phenomena. If you wish to experience spirit worlds, you must find a way of working with the soul outside the physical body. Although this is difficult, it is possible today for you to experience the spirit world while outside the body. Moreover, it is always possible to assess the spiritual observations of others. Those who are unable to make such observations themselves can use sound human reason to judge those of others—not the kind of reason usually called sound, but truly sound thinking. We are going to speak of how the human soul emerges from the physical body, on the one hand, and how it enters the spirit world, on the other. Last week, we spoke of this from another perspective, but today I want to consider it from the standpoint of *imagination* knowledge. Thus, we will discuss many images that can be pursued further in your meditations. By doing this, you will see that this path of knowledge has great significance.

The spirit world can be entered, as it were, in three ways. The first is the *portal of death,* the second the *portal of the elements,* and the third the *portal of the sun.* Those who wish to take the entire path of knowledge must pass through all three entries.

The portal of death has always been described in every mystery teaching. The portal of death can be attained only if we try to reach it through meditation—that is, complete surrender and devotion to certain thoughts or perceptions. These must be suited to your individuality and placed so entirely in the center of your consciousness that you identify with them completely. Human effort, of course, weakens very easily along this path, because there truly are necessary inner obstacles to be overcome. It is a matter of repeating, again and again, silent inner efforts to devote yourself so completely to the thoughts that you forget the whole world, living wholly in those thoughts.

With constant repetition, you gradually begin to sense that those thoughts at the center of consciousness are assuming a kind of independent life. You get the feeling that, up to this point, you have only "thought" the thought and placed it at the center of your awareness. Now, however, it begins to develop a life and inner agility of its own. It is as though you were able to produce a real being within yourself. The thought begins take on an inner structure. This is an important moment; you feel as though you envelop the thought. You realize that your efforts have enabled you to provide a stage for something to develop and now, through you, come into a life of its own.

Enlivened thinking is very significant for one's life of meditation. You become deeply stirred by the objective reality of the spirit world; you know that the spirit world, so to speak, is concerned with you and that it has approached you. Of course, getting to this moment is not simple, because you must first experience various sensations that you would not normally be inclined to go through. One is a certain feeling of isolation, loneliness, being forsaken. You cannot take hold of the spirit world without having had this feeling of being deserted by the physical world. It is a feeling that this physical world does many things that crush and wear you down. But we must come through this feeling of isolation, so that we can also bear the inner animation of awakened thought that emerges. You are confronted by resistance; from within yourself, there is a great deal of resistance to a real perception of this inner awakening of thought life.

One feeling in particular arises: an inner resistance to a feeling you would rather not go through. One cannot admit this, however, and instead might say, "I can never do this; it puts me to sleep; my thinking and inner flexibility desert me and refuse to go on." In other words, you feel compelled to invent all sorts of excuses to evade the necessary experience—that the enlivened thought acquires substance. It becomes substantial and forms a kind of being. Then you not only have the feeling, but also a vision, that the thought is, to begin with, like a little round seed that germinates into a being with definite form. From outside your head, it passes inside and makes you aware that you have identified with it, that you are inside the thought, and now you extend with the thought into your own head; but, essentially, you are also still outside. The thought assumes the form of a winged human head, flowing out into infinity, and extending back into your body through the head. The thought thus becomes a winged angel's head.

You must actually attain this. This experience is difficult, so we like to think that, at the moment the thought develops in this way, we can no longer think. It seems we will be taken at this moment. The body we have always known, and into which the thought extends, is experienced as a deserted automaton. In addition, in the spirit world there are all kinds of obstacles that prevent us from seeing this. This winged angel's head does become visible inwardly, but there is every conceivable hindrance to seeing it.

At this point, you have reached the threshold of the spirit world. But now you are confronted by the power we have always called Ahriman, although you do not see him at first. It is Ahriman who hinders us from seeing what I have described as a germinating thought being. Ahriman does not want you to see this and tries to hinder you. Because you reach this point primarily on the path of meditation, if you cling to the preconceptions of the physical world, it becomes easy for Ahriman to veil what you must achieve. In fact, you will admit that you cannot imagine how much you cling to the preconceptions of the physical world; neither can you imagine that there is another world whose laws are different from those of the physical world. I cannot list all the prejudices that people bring to the threshold of the spiritual world, but I will mention one of the primary and more intimate ones.

People speak of the physical world from a monistic worldview, as a unity. They repeatedly say that they can grasp the world only by contemplating it as a unity. We have had to go through strange experiences in this respect. A good many years ago, when the spiritual scientific movement began in Berlin with only a few members, there were several who felt they could not fully sympathize with it. One lady, for instance, came to us after a few months and said that spiritual science was not for her, because it required too much thinking, and she found that thinking wiped out everything precious for her and caused her to fall into a kind of sleep. In addition, she said that there is only one thing of real value, and that is unity. The unity of the world that a monist seeks in so many areas (and not just materialistic ones) had become a fixed idea with her. Unity, unity, and more unity. That was her quest.

In German culture we have the philosopher Leibnitz, an emphatically monistic thinker who did not seek unity but the many *monads,* which to him were essential units of soul.[1] It was clear to him that in the spirit world there could be no unity, only multiplicity. There are monists and pluralists. Monists speak only of unity and oppose the pluralists, who speak of multiplicity. But, in fact, both unity and multiplicity are concepts that are useful only in the physical world, but people believe that they must have value in the spirit world as well. But this is not so. People must see that, although unity can be glimpsed, it must be superseded immediately, because it reveals itself as multiplicity. It is both unity and multiplicity. Nor can ordinary calculation or any physical mathematics be transferred into the spirit world.

One of the strongest and, at the same time, most subtle Ahrimanic temptations is the desire to carry concepts acquired in the physical world into the spirit world, just as they are. We must approach the threshold without "baggage," without being weighed down by what we learned in the physical world; we must be ready to leave everything at the threshold. All concepts—exactly the ones we worked hardest to acquire—must be left behind, and we must be prepared to acquire new concepts in the spirit world; we will become conscious of something entirely new. Attachment to things of the physical world is extremely

---

1. Gottfried Wilhelm Leibnitz (1646–1716), philosopher and mathematician who fought with Isaac Newton over which of them had invented integral and differential calculus. He died with little recognition and few of his works published.

strong in people. They would like to take everything they have won in the physical world. But people must be able to approach a completely clean slate—complete emptiness—and allow themselves to be guided only by the thoughts that now begin to come to life. Basically, this entry into the spirit world has been called the "gate of death," because it is truly a greater death than the physical one. In physical death, you are persuaded to give up the physical body; but when entering the spirit world, we must resolve to give up our concepts, notions, and ideas and allow our being to be rebuilt.

Now you confront that winged thought being I mentioned. You can confront it even now by giving all your effort to living within a thought. All you need to know is that you must stand firm and not retreat when the moment comes that makes claims upon you that are different from any you have imagined. Retreat, in most cases, is subconscious. We become weak, but this is only the sign that we do not wish to give up our baggage. The whole soul and everything it has acquired on the physical plane must perish before entering the spirit world. This is why it is appropriate to call this the portal of death. You then look through the winged thought being, which is like a new spiritual eye you acquire, or through a spiritual ear—we also hear and feel—and thus become aware of what the spirit world holds.

It is even possible, my dear friends, to speak of specific experiences that you can have when entering the spirit world. To be able to have these experiences, you need only persevere in the methods of meditation I described. It is especially important to understand very clearly that certain experiences that you bring to the threshold of the spirit world must be put aside before entering. Experience tells us that the spirit world that will confront you is usually different from what you would prefer. This is the first portal, the portal of death.

The second portal now is the portal of the elements. This will be the second portal you pass through if you give yourself up to meditation with vigorous, sustained effort. But it is also possible for you to encourage your organization in such a way that you can actually reach the second portal without having passed through the first. This is not the best thing for a real knowledge, but it may happen that you reach this point without first going through the first portal. Truly appropriate knowledge will yield only itself if you pass through the first portal and then approach the second one consciously.

The second portal shows itself in this way: if you have passed through the portal of death, at first you sense that you have entered conditions that, outwardly, resemble sleep, though inwardly they are very different. Outwardly, you seem to be asleep so long as these conditions last. As soon as the thought begins to stir and grow, your outer self appears to be asleep. You need not be lying down—you may sit—but it is similar to sleep. Outwardly, it is impossible to distinguish, but inwardly it is absolutely different. Not until you return to normal life do you realize that you were not asleep but living in thought, just as you are now awake in the physical world and seeing phenomena around you. But you also know that you are awake; you think, form thoughts, and connect them. But a short time before, in that other state, thoughts formed themselves. One approached the other, explained the other, separated from the other, and what you usually do for yourself in thinking happened on its own. You also know that, whereas in physical life you are an I-being who adds thoughts together, in that other state you "swim" in one thought and then to another; you unite with thoughts; it evokes a feeling that space simply no longer exists.

It is no longer like physical space, where you go to a certain place and look back, and then go farther—and if you want to return to where you began, you would have to travel the road in reverse. Here you would have to make the same journey in both directions. This is not the case in that other state, in which space is different; you "spring" through space. At one moment you are in one place, the next somewhere far away. One does not pass through space—the laws of space have ceased. You now live and move within thoughts themselves. We know that the I is not dead; it weaves in a web of thoughts. But although we live in those thoughts, we do not immediately master them; the thoughts form themselves, and we are pulled along. We do not swim on our own in the stream of thoughts, but the thoughts take us on their "shoulders" and carry us along.

This state must also end, which it does when we pass through the portal of the elements. The whole process becomes subject to our will, and we can now follow a specific line of thought intentionally. We live in the entire life of thought with our volition. Again, this is a moment of tremendous importance. Consequently, I have even referred to it exoterically in public lectures by saying that we reach the second stage by identifying with our destiny. Thus, we acquire the power to be within the weaving thoughts through our own volition.

Now you can understand the essentials. If you have first passed through the gates of death, you are outside the body and can use only external forces of will. You must insert yourself into the cosmic harmony. The forces that you must use outside the body are also within you, but they function on an unconscious level. The forces that circulate your blood and make your heart beat come from the spirit into which we plunge when we immerse ourselves in the volitional element. Initially, when you passed through the portal of death, you are in a spirit world that does as it pleases with you. You learn to act for yourself in the spirit world by identifying with your destiny. This can be accomplished only gradually. Thoughts acquire being identical to your own. The acts of our being enter the spirit world. But to achieve this in the right way, you must pass through the second portal.

With the power you gain by identifying yourself with your destiny, you begin to weave in the thoughts in such a way that they do not carry you along in a dream-like way, but you are able to eliminate one thought and call up another, manipulating them at will. When this begins, you experience what we call "passing through the portal." Then the power of volition we are using reveals itself as a terrible monster. This has been known for thousands of years among mystics as "encountering the lion." You must go through this encounter. In your feeling life, this leads to dread—fear of what is taking place in the world of thought, fear of a living union with it. And this fear must be overcome, just as you had to overcome loneliness at the portal of death. This fear can, in manifold ways, simulate feelings that are not fear. But, in reality, it is a fear of what you are approaching.

Now you find the possibility of mastering this wild beast—the lion that meets you. In *imagination,* it appears as though it were opening its enormous, gaping jaws to devour you. The volition that you wish to use in the spirit world threatens to devour you. A constant feeling threatens to overcome you—that you are indebted to volition, but that you must also do or seize something. Nevertheless, you get a feeling about these elements of will within you: if you seize it, it will devour and eradicate you from the world. This is the experience of "being devoured by the lion." So (to speak of this in pictures), instead of surrendering to the fear that those will elements in the spirit world will seize, devour, and strangle you, you must swing onto the back of the lion, grasp the will, and use them for action. This is what you must do when this happens.

We have these forces within us. Therefore, if you are taken hold of by the will without having gone through the prescribed esoteric path—without having passed through the gate of death—you will also be seized by the forces that otherwise circulate your blood and beat your heart; then you do not use the forces outside the body but those within you. We could call this "grey magic." It would cause one to seize the spiritual world with forces we are not permitted to use for that purpose. The important thing is to see the lion—the monster before you—and to know what it looks like and how the forces of will wish to take hold of you. They must be mastered from outside the body. If you do not approach the second portal or perceive the lion, you will always be in danger of wanting egoistic power over the world. This is why the true path of knowledge leads us, first, from within the physical body and physical existence, and then to the conditions that should be met with outer essences.

On the other hand, most people are inclined to enter the spirit world by a more comfortable way than through true meditation. Consequently, it is possible to avoid the gate of death, and, if the inner predisposition is favorable, to approach the second portal directly. One can do this by giving oneself up to a particular image, an especially passionate image of dissolving oneself in the universal all or whatever—something recommended in good faith by certain false mystics. By this means, the efforts of thinking are dulled and the emotions stimulated—whipped into a fiery enthusiasm. In this way, one can, to begin with, be admitted to the second portal and be given over to the forces of will. Such a person does not master the lion, but is devoured, and the lion does as it likes. This means that occult events are taking place, but they are essentially egoistic. This is why we can never describe an experience that is stirred to a fury as simply a mystical feeling (although one might say there is also a risk of this in true esotericism today). This appeal to what stimulates people inwardly—whipping them out of the physical body but leaving them connected to the forces of the physical forces of the blood and the heart—no doubt leads to a kind of perception of the spirit world, and it may have much good in it. However, it will cause you to grope about insecurely in the spirit world, making it impossible to distinguish between egoism and altruism.

This brings us directly (if one must emphasize this) to a difficult point. With respect to true meditation and everything related to it, modern minds have mostly fallen asleep. People do not like to exert their thinking to the degree necessary if they are to identify with the thinking. They much prefer to be instructed to lovingly surrender to the cosmic spirit or the like, whereby the emotions are whipped up and thinking is avoided. People are thus led to spiritual perceptions, but without full awareness of them, and they are unable to distinguish whether the things they experience spring from egoism. Certainly, enthusiasm in feeling and perception must run parallel to selfless meditation, but thought must go with it; thinking must not be eliminated. Certain mystics, however, try to suppress thinking altogether, surrendering completely to a glow of frenzied emotion.

This, too, is a difficult point, because this method can be useful. Those who stimulate their emotions progress much more quickly. They enter the spirit world and have all sorts of experiences, and this is what most people want. The question for most people is not whether they enter the spirit world in the correct way, but whether they enter it at all. The problem is this: If we do not go through the gate of death first, but go directly to the

156 of ESOTERIC DEVELOPMENT

gate of the elements, at that point Lucifer prevents us from truly perceiving the lion. As a result, before we know it, we have been devoured. The difficulty is that we can no longer distinguish between what is related to us and what is outside in the world. Without passing through the gate of death, you can become acquainted with spirit beings or elementals and learn to recognize a rich, vast spirit world, but the spirit beings are, for the most part, those whose purpose is to maintain human blood circulation and the work of the human heart. Such beings are always around us in the spiritual, or elemental, world. They are spirits whose life element is in the air, in the encircling warmth, and in the light; their life element is in the music of the spheres, which is no longer physically perceptible. Such spirit beings weave through every living thing.

Naturally, we then enter this world. It becomes alluring, because one can make the most wonderful spiritual discoveries in this world. One who has not passed through the gate of death but goes directly to the portal of the lion, without seeing the lion, perceives an elementary spirit whose purpose is to maintain the heart's activity. Such an elementary spirit also maintains the heart activity of others and may, under certain circumstances, bring information of other people—even those of the past—or, perhaps, prophesy the future. This experience may be met with great success, yet it is not the correct path, because it does not leave us free in the spirit world.

The third portal that you must pass through is the portal of the sun. Once you reach this portal, you go through yet another experience. While at the portal of death, you perceived a winged angel's head; while at the portal of the elements, you perceived a lion; now, at the portal of the sun, you must perceive a fierce dragon—and you must truly perceive it. Lucifer and Ahriman, however, join in an attempt to make it invisible to your spiritual vision. Once you perceive it, however, you recognize that, in fact, that fierce dragon is fundamentally related to you. It is woven from the instincts and sensations of what we refer to as our lower nature in ordinary life. The dragon is made up of all the forces that, for example, one uses for digestion and many other functions. The forces of digestion and many other functions of our lower nature appears in the form of a dragon. You must contemplate the dragon as it coils out of you. The dragon is anything but beautiful. Thus it is easy for Lucifer and Ahriman to influence your subconscious soul life in such a way that, unconsciously, you avoid looking at the dragon. Also woven into the dragon are your absurdity, vanity, pride and selfishness—all your basest instincts.

This gate is called the portal of the sun, because the forces that form the dragon are in the sun forces, and it is the sun's forces that enable us to digest and accomplish other organic processes; this occurs, in fact, through living with the sun. If you fail to contemplate the dragon at the portal of the sun, you will be devoured and united with the dragon in the spirit world. You will no longer be distinct from the dragon—you experience the spirit world as the dragon. The dragon may have very significant and, in a sense, grand experiences that are more interesting than those at the portal of death or beyond it. Your experiences at the portal of death are at first colorless, shadowy, and intimate—so light and intimate that they may easily escape notice—and one is not at all inclined to be attentive enough to hold on to them. You must continually exert yourself to allow what comes easily as thoughts to expand. Ultimately, it expands into a world, but long, energetic effort is needed before that world appears as a reality, permeated with color, sound, and life.

Now you must let the colorless and soundless forms take life from infinity. If, for example, you discover a simple air or water spirit through what we might call "head clairvoyance" (which arises from the animation of thinking), that spirit initially flits away so lightly and quickly over the spiritual horizon that it does not interest you at all. If the air or water spirit is to have color or sound, it must be drawn to it from the whole sphere of the cosmos, which happens only with long inner effort and after you are blessed.

Just imagine—pictorially speaking—one of those air spirits: before it can approach in color, the color must flow into it from a powerful part of the cosmos. You must have the power to make those colors "shine in." This power, however, can be acquired only through devotion; radiating forces must pour in through devotion. If you are united with the dragon, however, when you see an air or water spirit you will be inclined to radiate the forces within you—forces from what we usually call the lower organs. This is much easier. The head is, in itself, a perfect organ, but in the astral and ether bodies of the head, there is little color, because colors are used up when forming the brain, for example, and especially the skull. When we approach the threshold of the spirit world and, in head clairvoyance, draw the astral and ether bodies out of the physical body, there is not much color in them. The colors were expended in forming the perfected organ, the brain.

When, however, we draw the astral and ether bodies out of the stomach, liver, gall-bladder, and so on through "belly clairvoyance," the colors have not been used to form perfected organs; those organs are only on the way to perfection. Beautiful colors come from the astral and ether bodies of the stomach; they gleam and glitter in every possible radiant hue. And if the ether and astral bodies are drawn out of these organs, the forms you see are imbued with wonderful colors and sounds. Therefore, one might see wonderful things and draw a picture with gorgeous colors. This would certainly be interesting, just as it is interesting for an anatomist to examine the spleen, liver, or intestines—from the perspective of science, this is indispensable. But when these beautifully colored pictures are examined by someone with experience, what appears is the underlying processes of digestion two hours after eating.

One certainly cannot object to an investigation of these matters. Anatomists must do their job, and someday science will gain much by understanding the function of the ether body in digestion. But we must be very clear: if you do not connect this with the dragon—if you approach the portal of the sun without awareness, and if you unconsciously summon the etheric and astral forces of the belly into the dragon—you radiate it into clairvoyance and receive a truly wonderful world of images. The most beautiful and easiest of attainments does not initially come from the higher forces of head clairvoyance, but from belly clairvoyance. You must understand this. From the viewpoint of the cosmos, this is not vulgar in an absolute sense, but only in a relative sense.

To produce what is needed for our digestion, the cosmos must work with tremendously significant forces. What matters is that we do not succumb to errors or illusions but know what things are. It is extremely important to know that something very beautiful is merely the process of digestion. But if you think that some celestial world is being revealed by that image, you are simply wrong. No intelligent person will object to the cultivation of science based on such knowledge, but one does object to matters being put in a false light; this is our concern. It is possible, for example, that someone—perhaps a natural clairvoyant—will draw out the ether and astral bodies directly through a certain stage of the digestive processes. It is just good to know what is happening at such times.

Through head clairvoyance (whereby all the colors of the etheric and astral bodies are used to produce the wonderful structure of the brain), it is difficult to fill what is colorless and soundless with colors and sounds. But with belly clairvoyance, it is relatively easy to see wonderful things in the world. You must also learn to use the forces involved in this kind of clairvoyance. The forces of digestion are involved in a process of transformation, and you experience them correctly by continually learning to identify with your destiny. This is another ground for learning: what initially appeared as a flying angel's head must be traced back to the other element we dealt with, so that you are dealing not just with the forces of digestion, but also with the higher ones, which are involved with your karma, or destiny. If you identify with it, you succeed in promoting the spiritual entities you see around you, which are now inclined toward the colors and sounds flowing in from cosmic space. The spirit world becomes naturally concrete and stable—so "solid" that we do as well there as we do in the physical world.

There is one great difficulty at the portal of death: you get the feeling (which must be overcome) that, essentially, you are losing yourself. If, however, you have stretched yourself and have identified with the life of thought, you may, at the same time, be aware that you are losing yourself, but also finding yourself. This is the experience you have. You lose yourself when entering the spirit world, but you also know that you will find yourself again. You must make the transition—to reach the abyss, lose yourself in it, but trust that you will find yourself again there.

This is an experience you must go through; everything I have described is an inner experience you must go through. You must learn that events in the soul are important. It is as though you were obligated to see something; if you are shown the way by a friend, it is easier than thinking it through for yourself. You can achieve everything described here if you submit to constant inner effort and self-control through meditation, as described in *How to Know Higher Worlds* and in the second part of *An Outline of Esoteric Science*.

It is very important to learn how to go through these foreign experiences beyond the threshold of the spirit world. It is natural for people, out of sheer need, to imagine the spirit world as a mere continuation, or duplication, of the physical world, but if you expect the spirit world to look like the physical world, you will be unable to enter it. All of your experiences there will be the reverse of those in the physical world. In the physical world, for example, people are accustomed to using their eyes to receive impressions by way of light. In the spirit world, however, it would be a mistake to think you can open spiritual eyes and receive impressions of light; you could not even enter there, because your expectations would be false. Something like a fog would weave around your spiritual senses, hiding the spirit world, just as a mass of fog conceals a mountain. In the spirit world, you cannot see objects illuminated by light—on the contrary, you must understand that you, yourself, stream with light into the spirit world. In the physical world, when light falls on an object, we see it; but in the spirit world, we are within that ray of light ourselves, and in this way we "touch" the object. In the spirit world, you know that you shimmer with a ray of light; you knows that you are within streaming light.

This knowledge can lead to concepts that help us progress in the spirit world. For example, it is very useful to imagine what it would be like to be inside the sun right now. Because we are not, we see objects illuminated by sunlight. But imagine being within the sunlight, thus touching objects from within the light. This "touch" is what we experience in the spirit world; indeed, experience there is knowing that you are alive in that world. You know that you are alive in the weaving thoughts. As soon as this condition begins, you become conscious of being within the weaving of thoughts, then comes a direct awareness of self-knowledge in luminous, streaming light. Thought belongs to light; it weaves in the light. You can experience this only when you are truly immersed in the light and in the weaving of thoughts.

Human beings have reached a stage where they must acquire these concepts; otherwise, they will pass through the gate of death into the spirit world and find themselves in very strange worlds. Our "stock," given to us by the Gods at the primal beginning of earth, has been gradually consumed. Human beings no longer have that ancient heritage to carry through the gate of death. People must gradually acquire the necessary concepts in the physical world—concepts that will serve after going through the gate of death, and make visible the tempting, seductive, dangerous beings we face there.

Spiritual science must be communicated to humanity today because of these great cosmic relationships. You can observe— even in our karma-laden time—that crossings are being created. People are passing through the gate of death in the prime of life. And, in obedience to the great demands of destiny, they have, in a sense, consciously allowed death to approach them in their youth. I am not talking so much about the moment before death on the battlefield, when there may be a great deal of enthusiasm, and the experience of death is not filled with the degree of awareness one prefers. But when the death has in fact occurred, it leaves behind an unspent ether body, on which the dead one can look back—this fact of death—with much greater clarity than would be possible if it had been the result of illness or old age.

Death on the battlefield is intense—an event whose effects are more powerful than any death caused by other means. It therefore affects the soul passing through the gate of death as an enlightenment. Death is terrible, at least for those who remain in the body. But once we have passed through the gate of death and look back at death, it becomes the most beautiful experience possible. Between death and new birth, looking back to our entry to the spirit world after death is the most wonderful, the most beautiful, the most glorious event possible. Little of our physical experience ever really remains as a memory of our birth; people do not remember physical birth with their ordinary, undeveloped faculties. Nevertheless, the phenomenon of death is always present to the soul that has passed through the gate of death, from the moment of the sudden emergence of awareness onward. It is always present, yet it stands there as a beautiful presence, an "awakener."

In the spirit world, death is the most wonderful teacher, one who can prove to a receptive soul that there is a spirit world, because, through its very being, it destroys the physical, and that destruction allows spirit to emerge. The resurrection of spirit, the complete stripping away of the physical, is an ever-present event between death and rebirth. It is a sustaining, wonder-filled event, and the soul gradually comes to understand it in a totally unique way, as though it is, in a sense, "self-selected"—not, of course, in the sense of those who seek their own death, but by having voluntarily considered it. When individuals, of their own free will, allow death to come to them, that moment acquires immense lucidity. Those who have not thus far thought much about death, or have had little concern about the spirit world, may find a wonderful teacher in their death. This connection between the physical and spirit worlds is very significant, especially during this war. I have emphasized this difficult time often; but the effects of mere teaching and words is not enough.

Great enlightenment is awaiting humankind in the future because there have been so many deaths. Those deaths work on the ones who have died, and the dead, in turn, work on the future development of human culture.

I can directly communicate to you certain words that came from one who recently passed through the gate of death in his early years—who "came through." For precisely this reason, these words are somewhat startling. They show that the one who experienced death with the clarity of a battlefield is now, within these alien experiences after death, working his way from earthly concepts toward spiritual concepts. I will communicate these words here. They are, if I may say so, intercepted by one who wanted to bring what the dying soldier would if he were able to return.

> Within the streaming
> Light I feel
> The life force.
>
> Death has waked
> Me from sleep,
> From spirit sleep.
>
> I will live on
> And do, out of myself,
> What the power of light
> Radiates into me.[2]

To a certain extent, this was what that suffering soul learned by looking back at his death. It was as though his being were filled with what must be learned by looking at death, and he wanted to reveal this information. "Within the streaming light I

---

2. "Im leuchtenden, / Da fhle ich / Die Lebenskraft. / Der Ted hat mich / Vom Schiaf erweckt, / Vom geistesschlaf. / Ich werde sein / Und aus mir tun, / Was Leuchtekraft / In mir erstrahlt."

feel the light force." He feels that he is more alive to understanding the spirit world than he was before death. He experiences death as an enlightener, a teacher: "Death waked me from sleep, from spirit sleep." And now he feels that he will be a doer in the spirit world: "I will live on and do, out of myself...," and he feels that his action comes from the forces of light within him; he feels the light working within him: "I shall live on and do, out of myself, what the power of light radiates into me."

One sees correctly that, everywhere, what we perceive in the spirit world gives us, again and again, the purest confirmation of what can become universal knowledge through *imagination* knowledge. This is what we would like to see properly revitalized through our spiritual scientific movement. We are not concerned merely with knowledge of the spirit world; such knowledge must become so alive in us that we adopt a new way of experiencing the world, so that the idea of spiritual science comes to life in us. It is this inner enlivening of the thoughts of spiritual science that (as I have repeatedly said) will be fundamentally demanded of us, so that it can be our contribution to the world evolution. This must be done so that the thoughts born of spiritual science, which soar into the spirit world as light forces, may unite with the radiant cosmos, and so that the cosmos may unite with what those who have passed through the gate of death in our fateful times wish to incorporate into the spiritual movement of culture. Then we will see the beginning of what these words imply:

> From the courage of fighters,
> From the blood on fields of war,
> From the suffering of the forgotten,
> From the people's sacrifice
> The fruits of spirit will flourish—
> When souls, conscious of spirit,
> Turn their senses toward the spirit world.

Bibliography & Further Reading

By Rudolf Steiner

THE ESSENTIALS OF ANTHROPOSOPHIC SPIRITUAL DEVELOPMENT

Intuitive Thinking As a Spiritual Path: A Philosophy of Freedom (1894), Great Barrington, MA: Anthroposophic Press, 1995. Rudolf Steiner lays out the prerequisites for a path of brain- and sense-free thinking as well as the epistemological foundations for his spiritual scientific observation. This work is also known as *The Philosophy of Freedom* and *The Philosophy of Spiritual Activity.*

How To Know Higher Worlds: The Classic Guide to the Spiritual Journey (2002), Great Barrington, MA: Anthroposophic Press, 1994. This is Rudolf Steiner's classic account of the modern path of initiation. He gives precise instructions for spiritual practice and descriptions of its results.

Theosophy: An Introduction to the Spiritual Processes in Human Life and in the Cosmos (1904), Great Barrington, MA: Anthroposophic Press, 1994. Steiner presents a comprehensive picture of human nature, beginning with the physical body, moving up through the soul to our spiritual being, with an overview of the laws of reincarnation and the working of karma. He describes a path of knowledge by which we can begin to understand the various ways we live in the worlds of body, soul, and spirit.

An Outline of Esoteric Science (1910), Great Barrington, MA: Anthroposophic Press, 1998. Originally intended to be a continuation of *Theosophy,* this work deals with the nature and evolution of humanity and the cosmos. It also extends and deepens much of what Steiner describes in *Theosophy.* It describes the path of knowledge, including the "Rose Cross meditation," complementing the descriptions in *Theosophy* and *How to Know Higher Worlds.*

A Way of Self-Knowledge (1912–1913), Great Barrington, MA: Anthroposophic Press, 1999. This volume begins with "The Threshold of the Spiritual World," a series of short, aphoristic descriptions of the world and human nature as seen with spiritual vision beyond the boundary between the sensory and spiritual realms. It is intended to present a few descriptions of certain spiritual experiences. From this perspective, these descriptions as well as those in "A Way of Self-Knowledge" should be considered supplementary to the other basic books; nevertheless, these descriptions stand on their own. The eight "meditations" in part two, "A Way of Self-Knowledge," unfolds in the reader and reveal the hidden inner forces that can be awakened in every soul.

OTHER WORKS BY RUDOLF STEINER

Anthroposophical Leading Thoughts: Anthroposophy As a Path of Knowledge, The Michael Mystery, London: Rudolf Steiner Press, 1998.

Anthroposophy (A Fragment): A New Foundation for the Study of Human Nature, Great Barrington, MA: Anthroposophic Press, 1996.

Anthroposophy and the Inner Life: An Esoteric Introduction, London, Rudolf Steiner Press, 1994.

Anthroposophy in Everyday Life, Great Barrington, MA: Anthroposophic Press, 1995.

At Home in the Universe: Exploring Our Suprasensory Nature, Great Barrington, MA: Anthroposophic Press, 2000.

Autobiography: Chapters in the Course of My Life, 1861–1907, Great Barrington, MA: Anthroposophic Press, 1999.

The Boundaries of Natural Science, Great Barrington, MA: Anthroposophic Press, 1987.

The Bridge between Universal Spirituality & the Physical Constitution of Man, Great Barrington, MA: Anthroposophic Press, 1958.

Christianity as Mystical Fact, Great Barrington, MA: Anthroposophic Press, 1996.

Correspondence and Documents, 1901–1925 (includes letters by Marie Steiner), Great Barrington, MA: Anthroposophic Press, 1988.

Cosmic Memory: Prehistory of Man and Earth, Great Barrington, MA: Steiner-Books, 1987.

The Effects of Esoteric Development, Great Barrington, MA: Anthroposophic Press, 1997.

First Steps in Inner Development, Great Barrington, MA: Anthroposophic Press, 1999.

Founding a Science of the Spirit, London: Rudolf Steiner Press, 1999.

Freud, Jung, & Spiritual Psychology, Great Barrington, MA: Anthroposophic Press, 2001.

From the History & Contents of the First Section of the Esoteric School, 1904–1914, Great Barrington, MA: Anthroposophic Press, 1998.

Guidance in Esoteric Training: From the Esoteric School, London: Rudolf Steiner Press, 2001.

Learning to See into the Spiritual World: Lectures to the Workers at the Goetheanum, Great Barrington, MA: Anthroposophic Press, 1990.

Love and Its Meaning in the World, Great Barrington, MA: Anthroposophic Press, 1998.

On the Life of the Soul, Great Barrington, MA: Anthroposophic Press, 1985.

Philosophy, Cosmology, & Religion, Great Barrington, MA: Anthroposophic Press, 1984.

A Psychology of Body, Soul, and Spirit: Anthroposophy, Psychosophy, Pneumatosophy, Great Barrington, MA: Anthroposophic Press, 1999.

The Reappearance of Christ in the Etheric, Great Barrington, MA: SteinerBooks, 2003.

Rosicrucian Wisdom: An Introduction, London: Rudolf Steiner Press, 2000.

The Secret Stream: Christian Rosenkreutz & Rosicrucianism, Great Barrington, MA: Anthroposophic Press, 2000.

Self-Transformation: Selected Lectures, London: Rudolf Steiner Press, 1995.

Sleep and Dreams: A Bridge to the Spirit, Great Barrington, MA: SteinerBooks, 2003.

The Souls' Awakening: A Mystery Drama, Great Barrington, MA: Anthroposophic Press, 1995.

The Spiritual Foundation of Morality: Francis of Assisi & the Christ Impulse, Great Barrington, MA: Anthroposophic Press, 1995.

The Spiritual Guidance of the Individual and Humanity, Great Barrington, MA: Anthroposophic Press, 1991.

Spiritualism, Madame Blavatsky, and Theosophy: An Eyewitness View of Occult History, Great Barrington, MA: Anthroposophic Press, 2002.

Start Now! Great Barrington, MA: SteinerBooks, 2003.

The Tension between East and West, Great Barrington, MA: Anthroposophic Press, 1983.

Truth and Knowledge: Introduction to "Philosophy of Spiritual Activity" Great Barrington, MA: SteinerBooks, 1981

What is Anthroposophy? Great Barrington, MA: Anthroposophic Press, 2002.

By Other Authors

Allen, Paul M. & Joan DeRis Allen, *The Time Is at Hand! The Rosicrucian Nature of Goethe's Fairy Tale of the Green Snake and the Beautiful Lily and the Mystery Dramas of Rudolf Steiner,* Great Barrington, MA: Lindisfarne Books, 1995.

Barnes, Henry, *A Life for the Spirit: Rudolf Steiner in the Crosscurrents of Our Time,* Great Barrington, MA: Anthroposophic Press, 1997.

Besant, Annie, H. P. Blavatsky, Mabel Collins, J. Krishnamurti, *Ancient Wisdom: At the Feet of the Master; Light on the Path; The Voice of the Silence,* Wheaton, IL: Quest Books, 1999.

Childs, Gilbert, *Rudolf Steiner: His Life and Work,* Great Barrington, MA: Anthroposophic Press, 1996.

Kühlewind, Georg, *From Normal to Healthy: Paths to the Liberation of Consciousness,* Great Barrington, MA: Lindisfarne Books, 1988.

———, *The Life of the Soul: Between Subconsciousness and Supraconsciousness,* Great Barrington, MA: Lindisfarne Books, 1990.

———, *Meditation for the Soft Will,* Great Barrington, MA: Lindisfarne Books, 2003.

———, *Stages of Consciousness: Meditations on the Boundaries of the Soul,* Great Barrington, MA: Lindisfarne Books, 1984.

———, *Working With Anthroposophy: The Practice of Thinking,* Great Barrington, MA: Anthroposophic Press, 1992.

Leivegoed, Bernard, *Man on the Threshold: The Challenge of Inner Development,* Stroud, UK: Hawthorn Press, 1985.

Lipson, Michael, *Stairway of Surprise: Six Steps to a Creative Life,* Great Barrington, MA: Anthroposophic Press, 2002.

Lowndes, Florin, *Enlivening the Chakra of the Heart: The Fundamental Spiritual Exercises of Rudolf Steiner,* London: Sophia Books, 1998.

Scaligero, Massimo, *The Light (La Luce): An Introduction to Creative Imagination,* Great Barrington, MA: Lindisfarne Books, 2001.

Sinnett, Alfred Percy, *Esoteric Buddhism,* 5th ed., Minneapolis: Wizards Bookshelf, 1973.

Smit, Jörgen, *Meditation: Bringing Change into Your Life,* London: Sophia Books, 1996.

Urieli, Baruch Luke & Hans Müller-Wiedemann, *Learning to Experience the Etheric World: Empathy, the After-Image, and a New Social Ethic,* London: Temple Lodge, 1998.

Notes on the Texts

1. "Esoteric Development," Berlin, December 7, 1905 (GA 54), translated by Gertrude Teutsch (revised).
2. "The Psychological Basis of Spiritual Science," lecture, Bologna, April 8, 1911 (GA 35), translated by Olin D. Wannamaker (revised).
3. "Supersensory Knowledge," from a series of lectures titled "Anthroposophy and the Human Inner Life," Vienna, September 26, 1923 (GA 84), translated by Olin D. Wannamaker (revised).
4. "The Attainment of Spiritual Knowledge," lecture, Dornach, September 20, 1922 (GA 344), translator unknown (revised).
5. "General Requirements for Esoteric Development," written for the esoteric school of the Theosophical Society in Germany (GA 245), translated by Charles Davy and Owen Barfield (revised).
6. "The Great Initiates," lecture, Berlin, March 16, 1905 (GA 53), translator unknown (revised).
7. "The Rosicrucian Spiritual Path," lecture, Berlin, October 20, 1906 (GA 96), translated by Diane Tatum (revised).
8. "Imagination Knowledge and Artistic Imagination," lecture, Berlin, October 21, 1906 (GA 96), translator unknown (revised).
9. "Three Decisions on the Path of Imagination Knowledge: Loneliness, Fear, and Dread," lecture, Berlin, March 2, 1915 (GA 157).

DURING THE LAST TWO DECADES of the nineteenth century the Austrian-born Rudolf Steiner (1861–1925) became a respected and well-published scientific, literary, and philosophical scholar, particularly known for his work on Goethe's scientific writings. After the turn of the century, he began to develop his earlier philosophical principles into a methodical approach to the research of psychological and spiritual phenomena.

His multifaceted genius led to innovative and holistic approaches in medicine, science, education (Waldorf schools), special education, philosophy, religion, agriculture (biodynamic farming), architecture, drama, movement (eurythmy), speech, and other fields. In 1924 he founded the General Anthroposophical Society, which has branches throughout the world.

FOR MORE ABOUT RUDOLF STEINER AND HIS WORKS, VISIT STEINERBOOKS ONLINE AT
www.steinerbooks.org